Scroll Saw Patterns for the Country Home

Patrick Spielman,
Patricia Spielman &
Sherri Spielman Valitchka

 Sterling Publishing Co., Inc. New York

Acknowledgments

Thanks to Dirk Boelman of The Art Factory for so excellently preparing the ink tracings of our drawings, quickly and perfectly. We also acknowledge with much gratitude the valuable help and assistance of our friend and typist, Julie Kiehnau, who also found time to cut out the projects pictured on the cover, as well as all the other projects in this book.

Library of Congress Cataloging-in-Publication Data

Spielman, Patrick E.
  Scroll saw patterns for the country home / by Patrick & Patricia Spielman and Sherri Spielman Valitchka.
    p.   cm.
  Includes index.
  ISBN 0-8069-0481-X
  1. Jig saws. 2. Woodwork. 3. House furnishings.
I. Spielman, Patricia. II. Valitchka, Sherri Spielman.
III. Title.
TT186.S67416 1993
684'.083—dc20   93-2329
                                        CIP

10 9 8 7 6 5 4

Published in 1993 by Sterling Publishing Company, Inc.
387 Park Avenue South, New York, N.Y. 10016
© 1993 by Patrick Spielman, Patricia Spielman & Sherri Spielman Valitchka
Distributed in Canada by Sterling Publishing
c/o Canadian Manda Group, P.O. Box 920, Station U
Toronto, Ontario, Canada M8Z 5P9
Distributed in Great Britain and Europe by Cassell PLC
Villiers House, 41/47 Strand, London WC2N 5JE, England
Distributed in Australia by Capricorn Link Ltd.
P.O. Box 665, Lane Cove, NSW 2066
Manufactured in the United States of America
All rights reserved

Sterling ISBN 0-8069-0481-X

Contents

Color section follows page 64.

Metric Equivalents

INCHES TO MILLIMETRES AND CENTIMETRES

MM—millimetres   CM—centimetres

Inches	MM	CM	Inches	CM	Inches	CM
⅛	3	0.3	9	22.9	30	76.2
¼	6	0.6	10	25.4	31	78.7
⅜	10	1.0	11	27.9	32	81.3
½	13	1.3	12	30.5	33	83.8
⅝	16	1.6	13	33.0	34	86.4
¾	19	1.9	14	35.6	35	88.9
⅞	22	2.2	15	38.1	36	91.4
1	25	2.5	16	40.6	37	94.0
1¼	32	3.2	17	43.2	38	96.5
1½	38	3.8	18	45.7	39	99.1
1¾	44	4.4	19	48.3	40	101.6
2	51	5.1	20	50.8	41	104.1
2½	64	6.4	21	53.3	42	106.7
3	76	7.6	22	55.9	43	109.2
3½	89	8.9	23	58.4	44	111.8
4	102	10.2	24	61.0	45	114.3
4½	114	11.4	25	63.5	46	116.8
5	127	12.7	26	66.0	47	119.4
6	152	15.2	27	68.6	48	121.9
7	178	17.8	28	71.1	49	124.5
8	203	20.3	29	73.7	50	127.0

Introduction

This is our second book of country designs for scroll sawing. This book features many all-new quick and easy patterns to make projects designed for those homes decorated with a country flavor. You'll find patterns for making functional objects and patterns intended purely for decoration. Use your imagination to interchange or combine the two types of patterns. Door/window topper patterns, for example, can be drawn to serve as the top design of a wider board sawn to make a pegboard or clothes rack. Use the same type of idea with the welcome sign patterns; they can be applied to wider backing. Then, just add some pegs and you've got a perfect clothes rack for your entry hall.

Other designs can be used to make simple storage boxes, wall shelves, benches, baskets, cutting boards, bulletin boards, and so on. Designs can be pierced or sawn through to give a silhouetted opening, or designs can be cut out, painted, finished and then glued onto a backing as an overlay. There's great potential for using the ducks and rooster segmented designs as overlays for name boards or welcome signboards, on cup racks, clothes racks, and tie racks, or on any plain plaque or backing material.

You'll find projects that use ready-made thermometers and clock inserts. Such projects could also be incorporated into many of the other cutout patterns. We suggest and encourage the reader to maximize the use of these patterns by considering all possibilities. All of the ideas contained herein, along with the additional possibilities created when you enlarge or reduce the patterns, will provide you with many more potential projects.

Because photocopiers are now so accessible to almost everyone, we've included some tips on how to use them quickly and efficiently to size a project to any dimension. You'll be able to custom size a pattern or design a pattern to fit your own needs. Newer photocopiers can enlarge an original by 200%, in one-percent increments.

Select natural woods and apply a painted or stained finish to match your own decorating and color schemes. We've tried to simplify the painting and finishing procedures so that beginners and first-time scroll sawers can duplicate or copy exactly what we've done, if the beginners aren't naturally creative, or if they feel inadequately artistic. Refer to the color pages, and use the photos of the painted projects as a guide when you paint your own country projects.

If scroll sawing is new for you, we recommend *Scroll Saw Basics* (see page 189); this book provides essential instructions for scroll saws and how to use them to make basic cuts.

Basic Tips

The country patterns and projects in this book are fun, fast, and essentially very easy to make. Making these cutouts requires no great artistic talents, no special equipment (other than a scroll saw) and no special sawing skills. (See Illus. 1.) Any boy or girl beyond the age of eight or nine can easily learn the fun of scroll sawing and he or she will soon be making these projects for themselves or for gifts. Many of the patterns can also be cut with a band saw, but youngsters and beginning woodworkers shouldn't use this machine without complete instruction and constant supervision. The scroll saw is much safer than the band saw, and it's easier for all to learn to use.

Sizing Patterns with a Photocopier

Most communities have photocopiers with enlarging capabilities; they're found in public libraries, banks and schools. Many print shops and specialized businesses ("copy shops") are found in most areas of the country. Check the business index of your telephone directory under the headings "photocopying" or "copying" for the nearest business specializing in this service. The cost to make a copy of a pattern from this book is minimal (usually just a few cents). Having a copy made is quick, convenient, and far more expedient and accurate than other old-fashioned ways of copying or enlarging patterns that used the squared grid system or pantograph tracings.

Enlarging with a Proportional Scale

Better-quality photocopiers enlarge or reduce pattern sizes in 1% increments. They can enlarge up to 200% of the original. A proportional scale is an inexpensive device that helps you to determine exactly what percentage of enlargement or reduction to set the photocopier to produce a specific-size pattern. The scale is very easy to use; all the little numbers and divisions make it look much more complicated than it really is. This device is simply two rotating discs with numbers around their perimeters joined by a common pivot. Align the number or dimension you have on one disc with the dimension you want on the other. The exact percentage to set the copy machine will appear in the opening.

To see how helpful this tool is, and how easy it actually is to use, enlarge a design that's 3⅜″ long to 5″ in length, by following the steps described in Illustrations 2 through 4. This process eliminates the guesswork and trial-and-error methods from the sizing process. This process also saves paper and money spent on wasted copies. Proportional scales are found in art, graphics, and printing-supply stores. Check the business section of your telephone directory to locate one of these helpful devices.

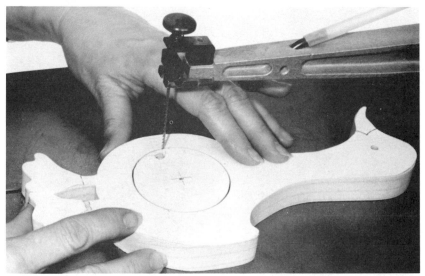

Illus. 1. Any small scroll saw can be used to make the projects in this book. Here ¾" stock is being cut following a paper copy of the pattern that's glued to the wood. The operator is sawing out an inside opening for a clock insert. Note the hole through which the blade was threaded to make this inside-opening cut.

Illus. 2. Here's the problem: Enlarge a pattern or part of a pattern (as shown) that's 3⅜" long to 5" long.

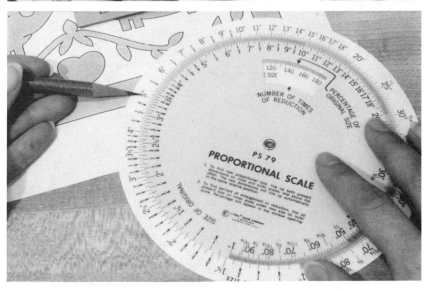

Illus. 3. Line up the 3⅜" marker of the inside disc to the 5" marker on the outside disc. Now read the exact percentage so you can set the copy machine to get a copy of the desired size. In this example, you'll get a 5"-long copy when the 3⅜" original is enlarged 148 percent.

Illus. 4. The enlarged copy is exactly 5" long, as desired.

Illus. 5. Use an aerosol temporary-bonding adhesive. Note that the pattern is scissor-cut to a rough size, and a newspaper catches the excess spray.

Illus. 6. After you've finished sawing the outline, remove the pattern. The paper should peel off easily without sticking or leaving any residue on the wood surface.

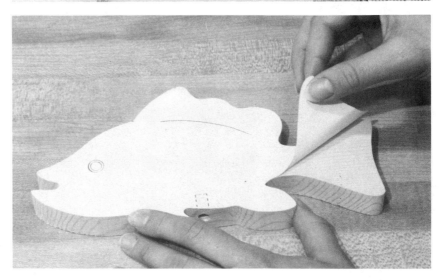

Wood Material & Thickness

Some of the patterns specify the kind and thickness of the material to use. However, with many projects, it really doesn't matter, thick or thin, solid softwoods or plywoods can all be good choices for specific projects. Many we made were sawn from No. 2 pine boards with parts cut from clear areas between knots and other defects. There are some projects that we think look great sawn from 1½"-thick material, but they can often be sawn (and still look good) from thinner stock. It's helpful to have access to ¼" plywood and ¼"-thick solid wood for some of the smaller projects. Thin plywoods are recommended for some hanging projects with ornate fret-type cutouts. Use solid woods for overlays, especially those overlays with hand-shaped, rounded edges.

Transferring Patterns to the Wood

Full-size patterns can be transferred to wood in several ways. Some people prefer to scissor-cut the pattern to a rough size and attach it directly to the wood. This can be done using rubber cement or special spray adhesives, as shown in Illus. 5. Spray a very light mist only to the back of the paper pattern. Don't spray directly onto the wood. Test the spray beforehand, using a small piece of paper and a small wood sample, to ensure that the pattern adheres well enough for cutting, yet peels off easily afterwards. See Illus. 6.

Patterns can also be transferred by scissor-cutting them to their final shape and carefully tracing them onto the wood, using a sharp pencil.

Some craftspeople may also prefer the traditional method of using carbon or graphite transfer paper to transfer a design to the workpiece. However, these two techniques are neither as easy nor as accurate as temporarily bonding a paper copy of the pattern onto the wood and then sawing through the pattern.

Finishing & Painting Details

All of the finishing materials and supplies we used were basic products (Illus. 7) that can be purchased at a local crafts shop, art supplier, or through one of the many mail-order houses. Not shown in the photo are various grades of sandpaper (80-, 100-, 120-, and 150-grit), some oil stains, wiping towels (or rags), plastic or rubber gloves and other easy-to-find supplies. Most of the solid-color paints and stains are easiest applied using foam brush-type applicators.

However, cotton rags, towels, and sponges make good applicators and wipes, too. Water-based acrylic paints are the easiest and safest to use. Premixed country paint colors are available in blues, reds, peach, cream (and so on), with each manufacturer designating its own color names. For example, one manufacturer names one of its "country" greens "Vermont Forest," dark, medium, or light, and so on.

Illus. 7. Typical finishing materials include white glue, water-based paint (acrylics), clear oil finishes, and painting pens for fine-line detailing. Foam brushes and small artist brushes are helpful, as are a tracing stylus and dotting tools (folk-art tools) shown at the right.

Illus. 8. Antiquing: To achieve an old look, partially wipe away a darker or lighter top coat before it dries, using a coarse-textured rag, like this piece of old towel.

Illus. 9. The sponging technique. Randomly dab on paint using applicators such as sponges, textured cloth, or crunched paper.

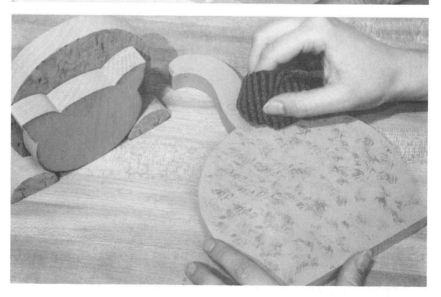

Antiquing

To make a piece look old, you could use a prepared antiquing overcoat, or you could use your own combination of colors (pre-tested on scrap). First apply any undercoat in the color you've chosen. Allow the undercoat to dry, and then spray the piece with a sealer. When the sealer dries, apply the antiquing paint in a color that contrasts with the undercoat, and then immediately wipe or sponge away the antiquing paints (Illus. 8) to get the streaking effect desired. When the piece is dry, apply water-based varnish or an acrylic sealer.

Another easy technique employed to make pieces look old and worn is to randomly sand through the finish at corners and edges. Sand to round slightly while exposing the raw wood or the contrasting paint base coat underneath. See the color section; technique has been used on several projects.

Sponging is an interesting technique often appropriate for large flat surfaces to make them look interesting. Randomly dab on paint of a color that contrasts somewhat with the base color, using sponges, textured cloth, crunched paper, or the like. See Illus. 9.

Spattering is a very simple process. Paint of one color is spattered over another color of the base coat by propelling droplets from a stiff bristle brush, as shown in Illus. 10. Mask any areas you don't want covered with the spattered paint. In the example shown, the eye and bill areas are masked with paper cut from the pattern. The paper was then pressed onto the wood surface.

Applying definition lines that represent facial features of eyes, or ears, or other details of animals or people is very easy to do, using paint pens, or felt-tip markers, or templates or other common drawing aids. See Illustrations 11, 12, 13, and 14.

Sometimes it will be necessary to trace-transfer the appropriate detailing directly from the pattern to the work surface. Do this after the object has been sawn out and then painted with the base or background coat. All patterns that have extra detailing should be removed from the workpiece very carefully and then kept intact after the initial profile has been sawn out. Save the pattern until you're ready to transfer the definition lines to the painted object.

Align the pattern again to the workpiece. The pattern may still have sufficient tack to help hold it in position, as shown in Illus. 15. Avoid using carbon paper for transferring pattern detailing; carbon paper is greasy, almost impossible to remove, and tends to bleed through painted surfaces. Graphite paper is a far better choice, and it won't give you all the problems carbon paper does. You can also use white or colored chalk, and apply it to the back of the pattern. See Illus. 16.

Decorative dots can be applied one at a time using the pointed end of an artist's brush handle, tracing stylus, or any similar object. Perfectly spaced dots in various patterns, and in any number, are easy to apply with the help of various dotting tools, as shown in Illus. 17. These tools are available from various hobby-supply stores and mail-order catalogs.

Refer to one of our other books, *Scroll Saw Country Patterns*, for more projects and other finishing tips.

Illus. 10. An old toothbrush makes a fine tool for giving small projects a "spattered" finish. Although it's hard to see in this photo, the eye and bill areas have been masked with a cut-up pattern.

Illus. 11. Here a draftsman's oval or ellipse template is used with a narrow-line paint pen or marker to draw/paint on a perfectly shaped eye. Note the small paper mask (that's been removed) which protected the eye area from the spatter finish.

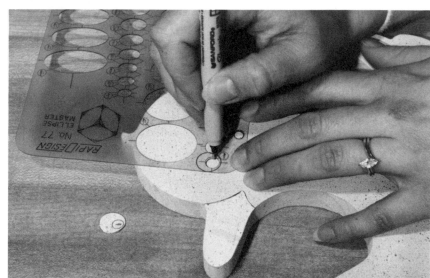

Illus. 12. The resulting perfect fine-line work defines the bill and eye.

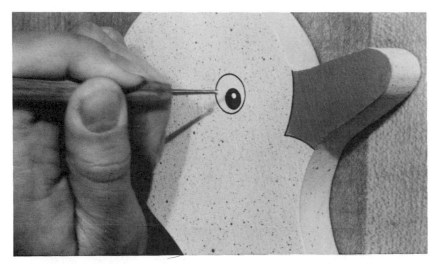

Illus. 13. Apply a white dot to the eye using the end of a tracing stylus (as shown), the end of a paintbrush or a pencil tip, loaded with paint. Practise first.

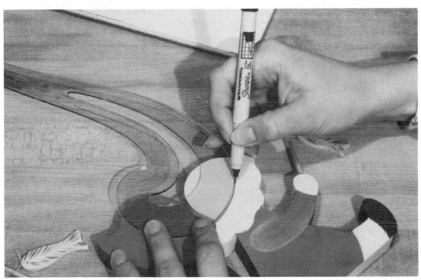

Illus. 14. A fine-point marker guided with a draftsman's french curve is used to "paint" smooth, long arches and curved detailing.

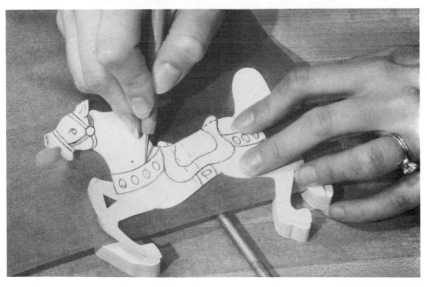

Illus. 15. The removed cut-out paper pattern is aligned again to the wood profile (just to the leg areas here) and pressed to steady it as the other details are traced, using a tracing stylus (or ballpoint pen) over graphite copy paper.

Illus. 16. With the detail lines transferred to the prepainted surface, trace the lines with paint pens.

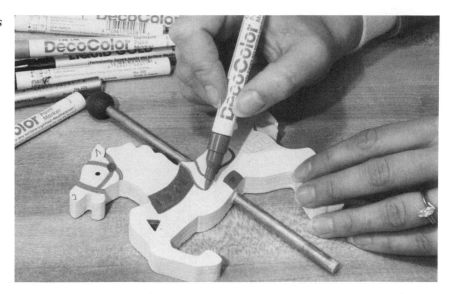

Illus. 17. Use a folk-art decorative dotting tool to make repetitive design to add interest to your painted detailing. Note the smooth curved lines, painted with the aid of a french curve.

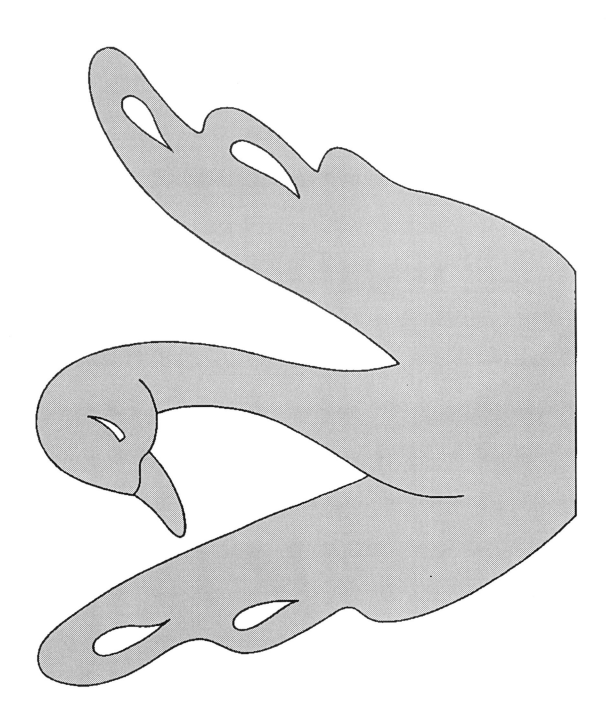

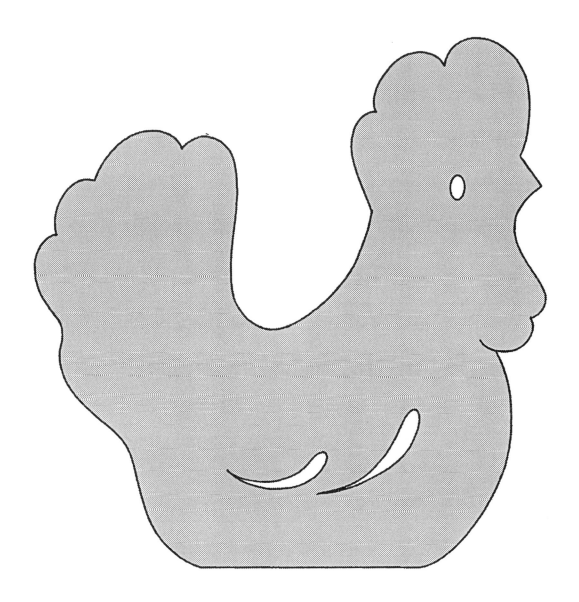

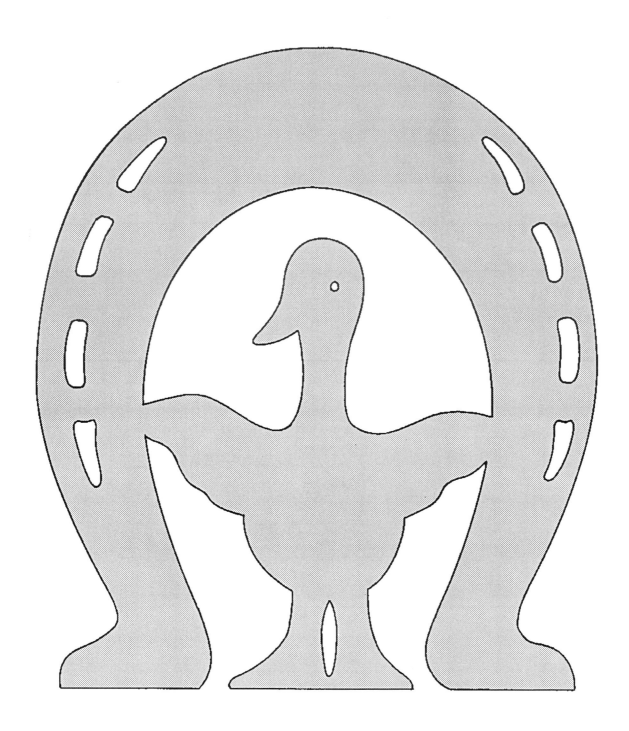

Horseshoe cutout with raffia bow. See page D of the color section.

Accordion cats, cut from ¼"- to ½"-thick material. See page D of the color section.

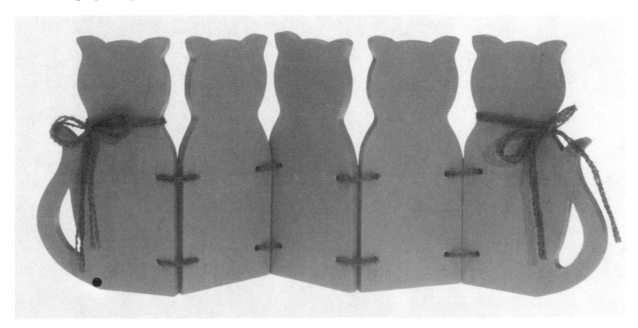

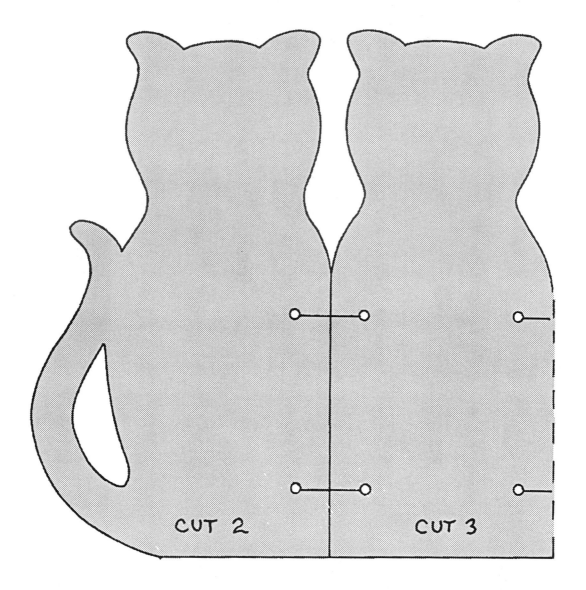

CUT 2

CUT 3

See page D of the color section.

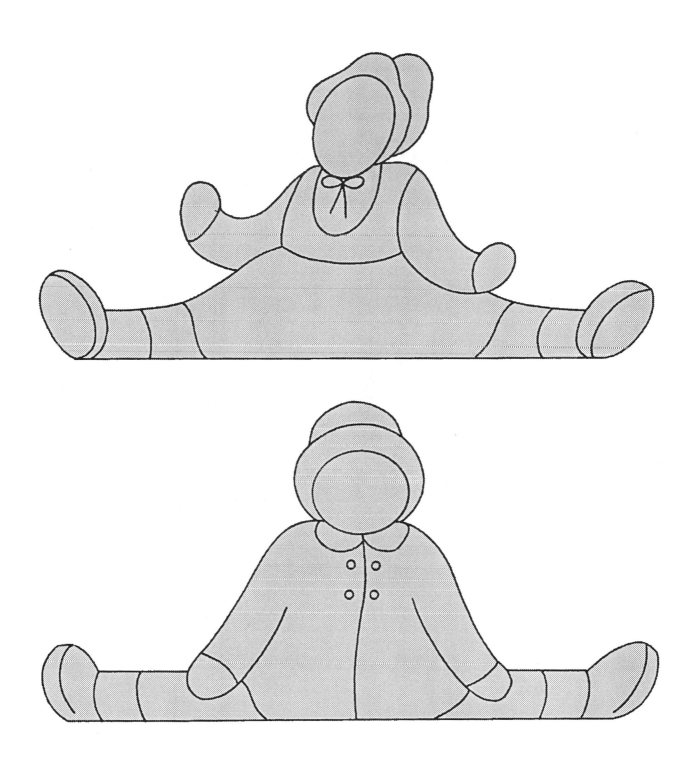

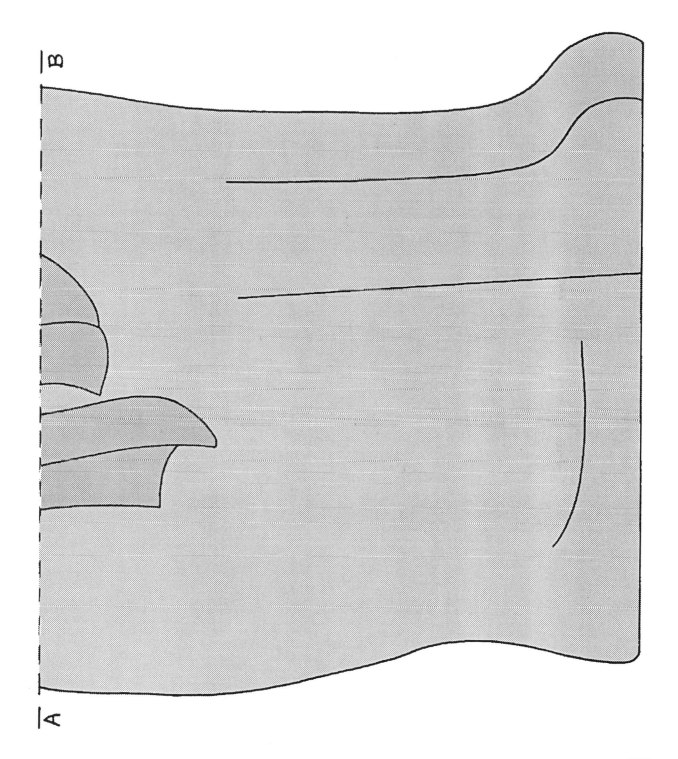

See page F of the color section.

28

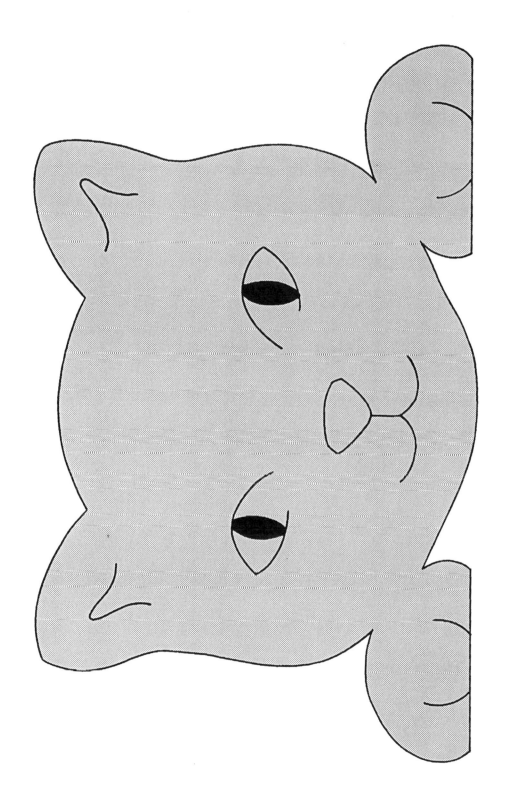

See the photos on page 32 and page G of the color section.

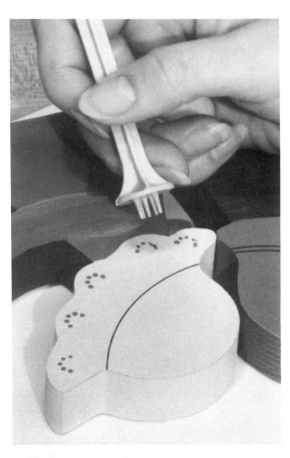

You could use a folk-art dotting tool to decorate the girl's hat.

Kids fishing. Cut from stock at least ¾"-thick, one piece or two. See page F of the color section.

Cutouts with Overlays

See the photos on page 32 and page G of the color section.

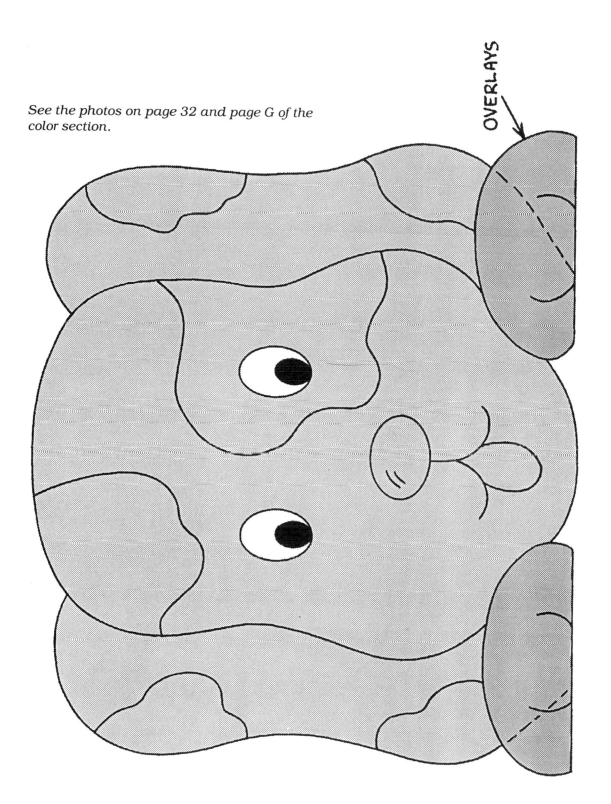

OVERLAYS

31

Cats and dog. Use 1" to 1½"-thick stock. See page G of the color section.

The small pig at left is two pieces. The large pigs in center are cut puzzle-style or they can be cut as overlays as seen on the right. See page A of the color section.

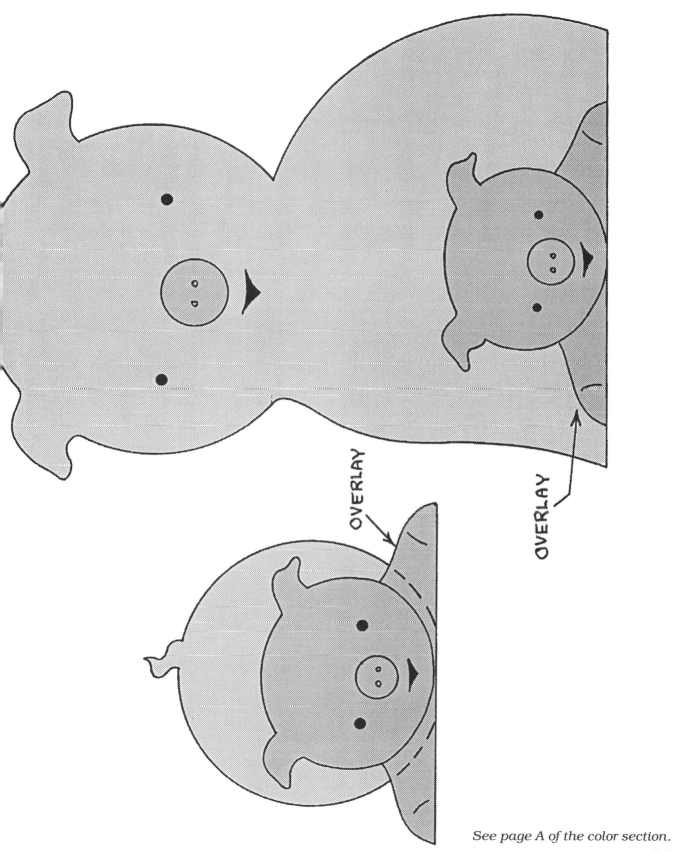

OVERLAY

OVERLAY

See page A of the color section.

See the photos on page 32 and page A of the color section.

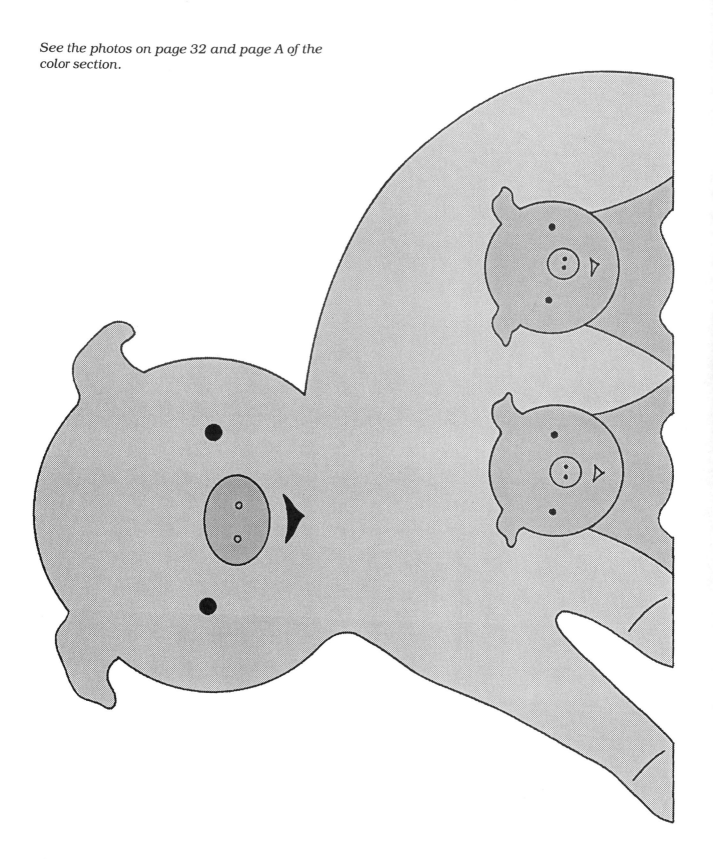

34

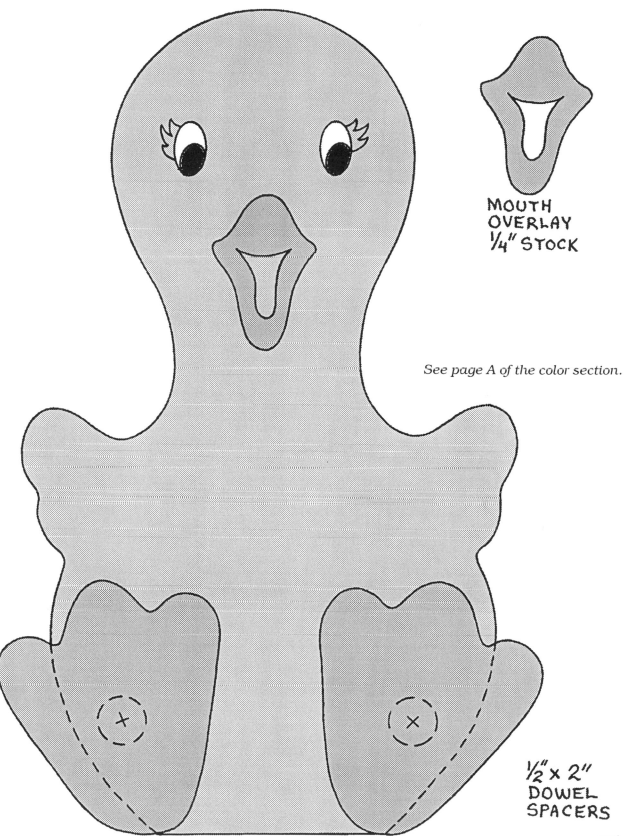

MOUTH
OVERLAY
¼" STOCK

See page A of the color section.

½" x 2"
DOWEL
SPACERS

35

Spatter-finished ducks. The feet are set away from the bodies by using dowels. See page A of the color section.

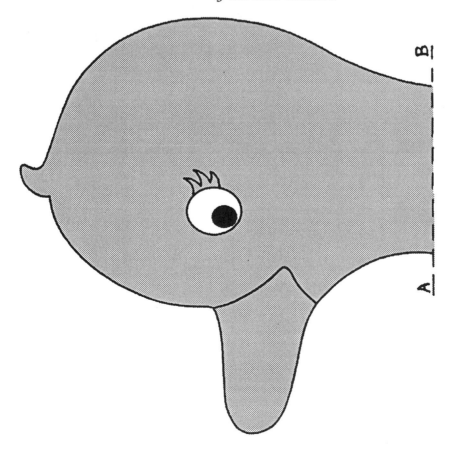

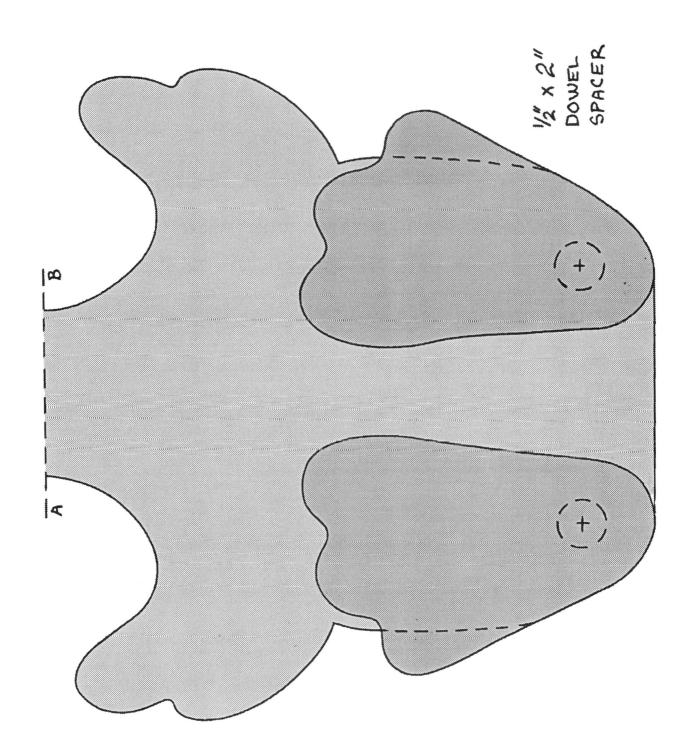

½" x 2"
DOWEL
SPACER

A

B

38

OVERLAYS

See page G of the color section.

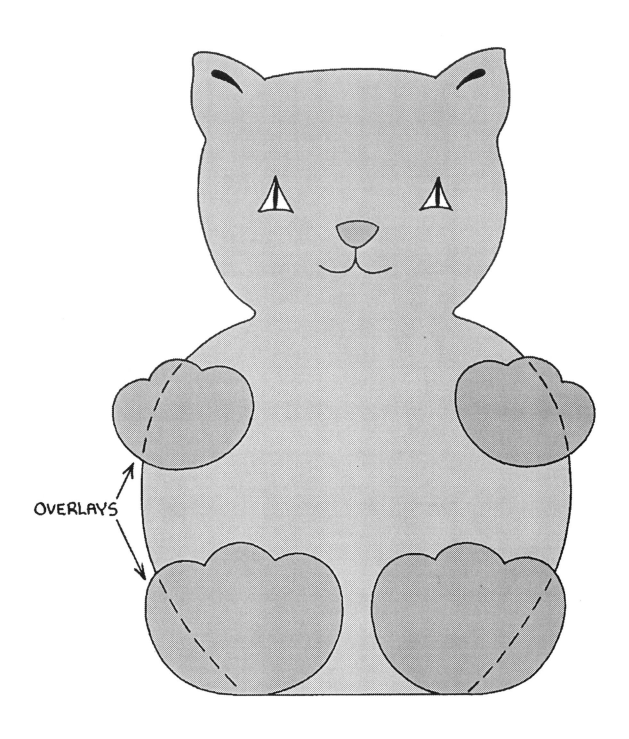

OVERLAYS

See page G of the color section.

Bear and cat with overlays. See page G of the color section.

"I Love You" bears with thin-stock overlays. See page F of the color section.

41

See page F of the color section.

A "Welcome" heart and an angel

OVERLAY

OVERLAY

See the photos on page 48 and page D of the color section.

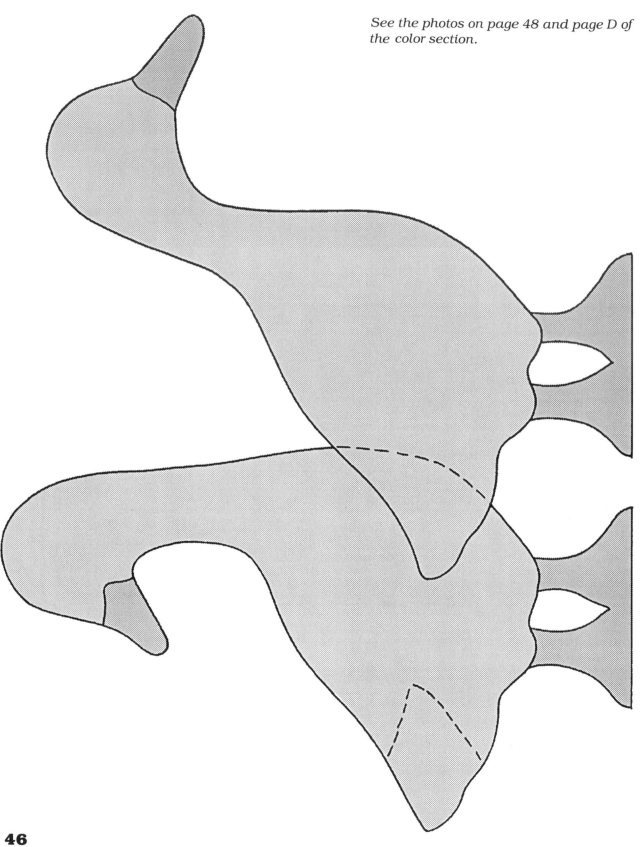

See the photos on page 48 and page D of the color section.

46

See the photos on page 48 and page D of the color section.

HEAD & LEGS
OVERLAYS

Four individual duck cutouts, glued one in front of the other. See page D of the color section.

A cow. Four legs and the face are glued to the body. See page D of the color section.

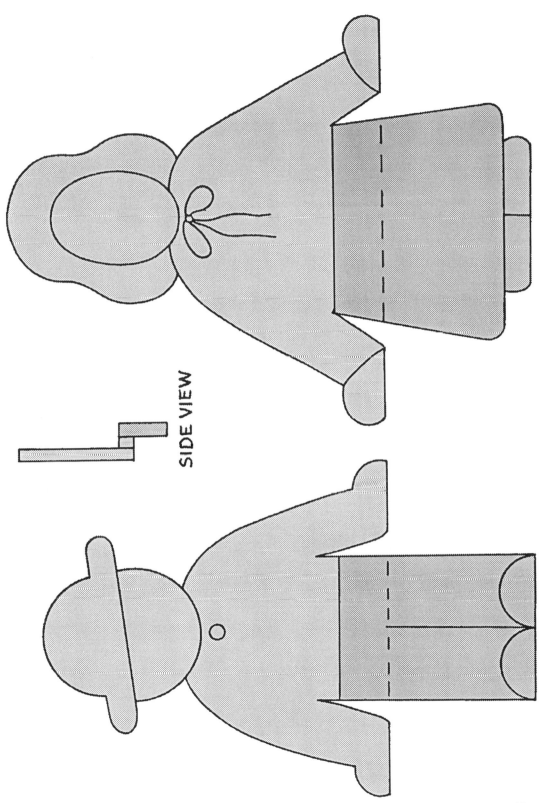

SIDE VIEW

Layered shelf-setting people

SIDE VIEW

Layered shelf-setting rabbit

50

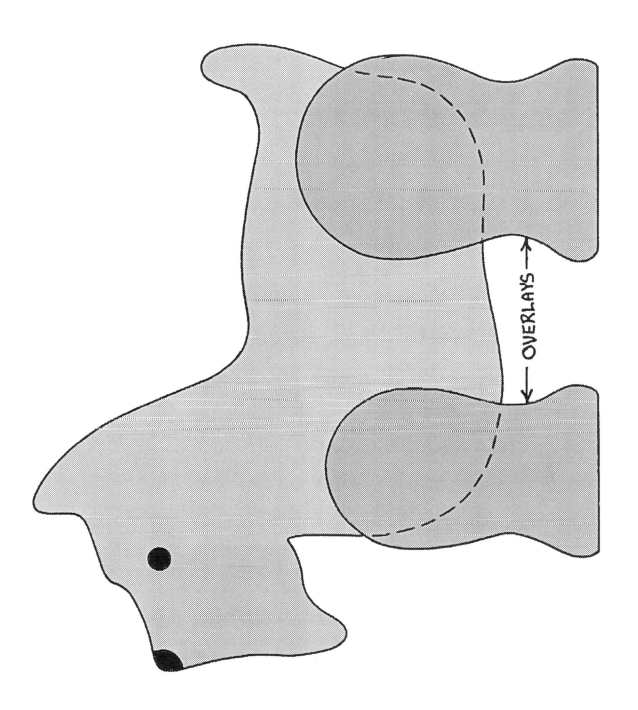

Scottie dog. Cut the wood to make four legs.

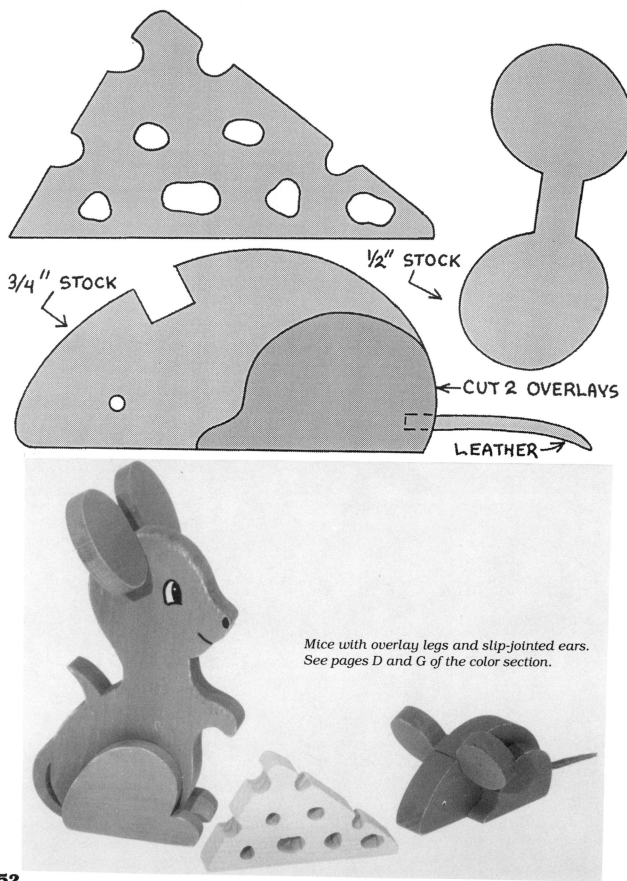

3/4" STOCK

1/2" STOCK

CUT 2 OVERLAYS

LEATHER →

Mice with overlay legs and slip-jointed ears.
See pages D and G of the color section.

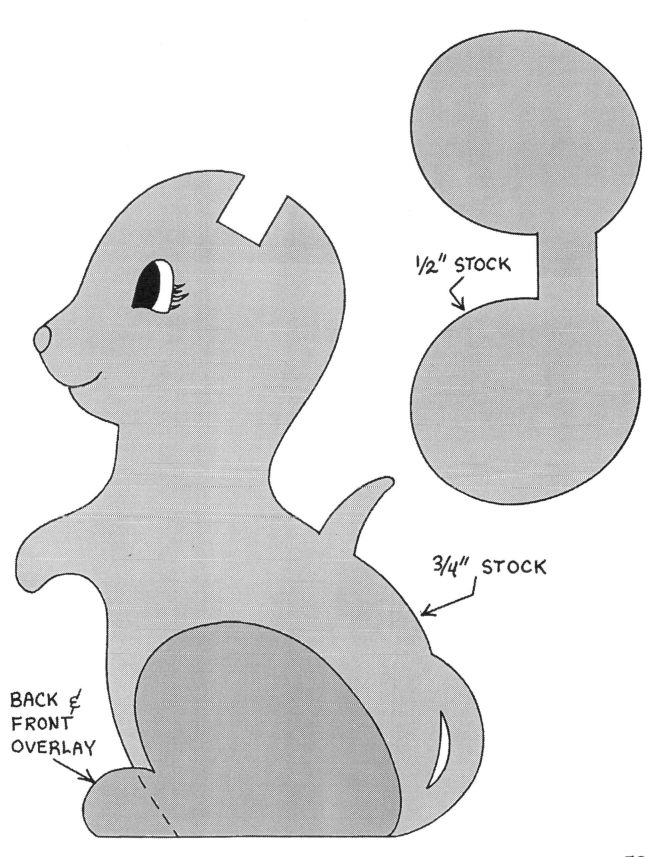

1/2" STOCK

3/4" STOCK

BACK &
FRONT
OVERLAY

*Four-layer animals. All pieces are cut from
¾"-thick stock. See page F of the color
section.*

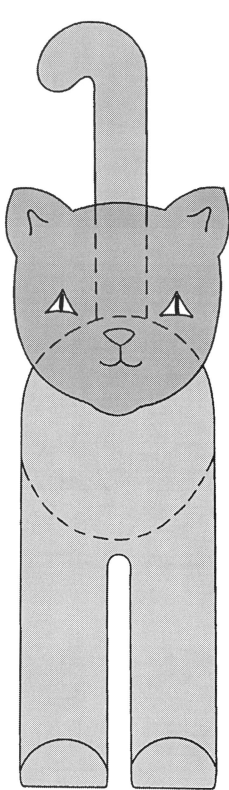

See the photos on page 58 and page C of the color section.

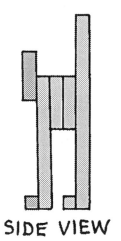

SIDE VIEW

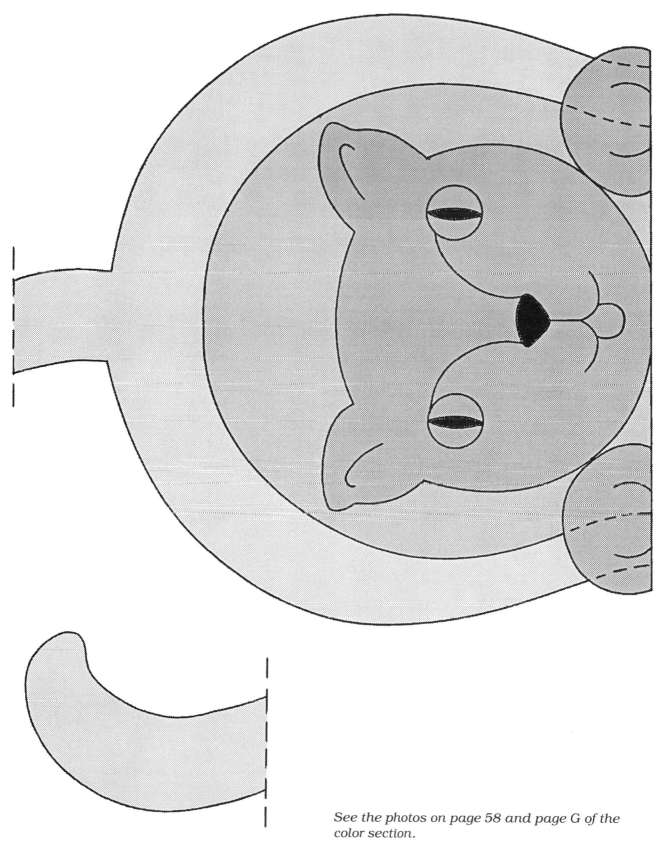

See the photos on page 58 and page G of the color section.

Five-layered tall cat. See page C of the color section.

Three-layered cat. The body layers are finished with the sponging technique. See page G of the color section.

58

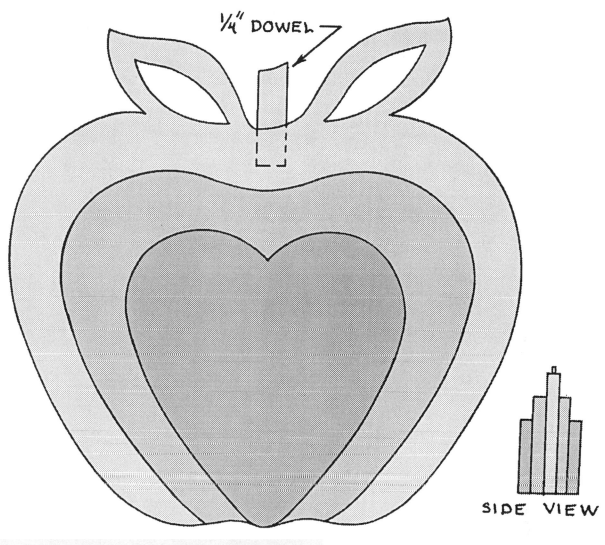

1/4" DOWEL

SIDE VIEW

Five-layered fruit. See the detail on the patterns.

59

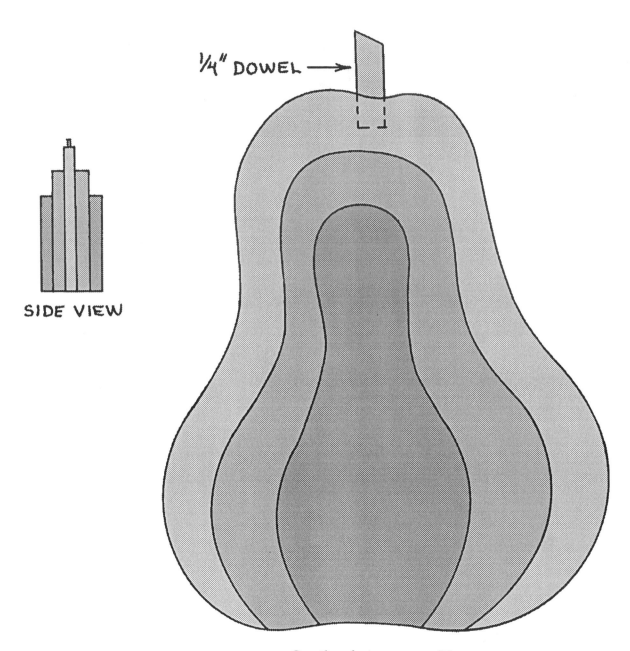

¼" DOWEL →

SIDE VIEW

See the photo on page 59.

Wire (or String) Hanging Projects

See the photos on page 62 and page H of the color section.

Hanging mobile. Use ¼" (or thinner) plywood.

Bear & pillow, done in ½"-thick cutout-puzzle style. Hearts and star are ¼" thick. See page H of the color section.

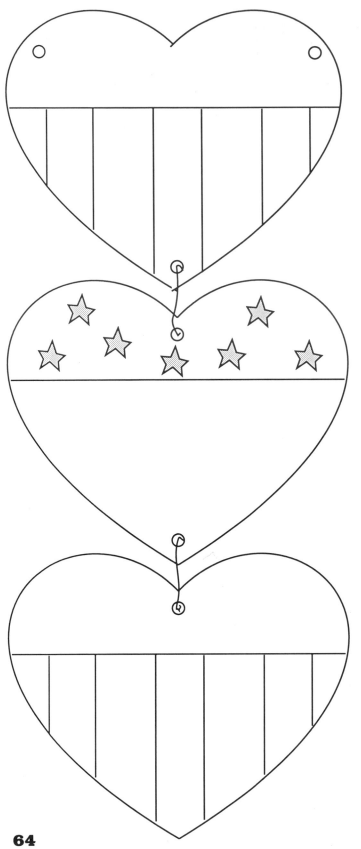
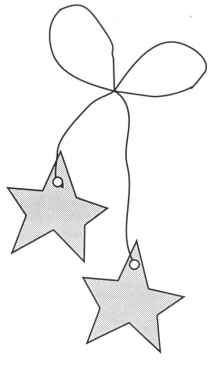
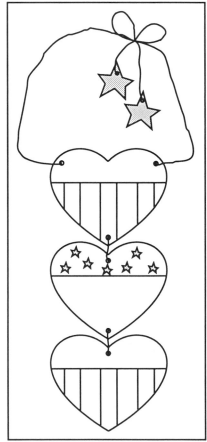

*An eye-catching
Noah's Ark coatrack
for any child's room
(See pages 138–140.)*

*Miniclocks can be fitted
into almost any country
cutout. (See page 160.)*

*What could be more country
than ducks and pigs? (See
pages 33–37.)*

A

These segmented projects are fun to make and they look spectacular anywhere. (See pages 93, 95, 97, 98.)

(Right) A pair of napkin holders (See pages 114–115.)

(Above) Visitors will admire these welcome signs.(See pages 100–103.)

(Left) Some colorful projects to brighten your kitchen (See pages 110, 111, 113, 118 and 119.)

B

*Symbols of country decor
(See pages 78, 81 and 82.)*

*(Left) A barn shelf for minia-
tures and a country-kitchen
clock (See pages 151 and
164.)*

*(Below left) A colorful
selection of pegboards
(See pages 133 and
136.)*

*This colorful birdhouse (below) is
perfect in any room. (See pages 56,
70, 71.)*

c

This duck shelf, perfect for the den, can be made in any length. Where did that mouse come from? (See pages 52 and 137.)

Typical country decorations (See pages 22, 24 and 47.)

A gaggle of geese, a cat, and a collector box for miniature cut-outs (See pages 45, 46, 129, 148, 149 and 150.)

D

Designs for door/window toppers and pegboards (See pages 122 and 123.)

(Left) Attractive window silhouettes and a wall plaque (See pages 173–175.)

(Below) Amusing frames for those special photos, with a carousel horse, a goose, and a teddy bear (See pages 90, 168 and 169.)

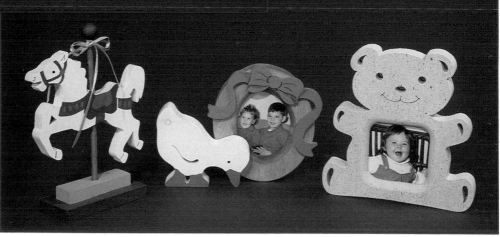

(Above) Love bears and kids fishing are fun and easy projects. (See pages 28 and 42.)

(Right) Wheeled animals with a rabbit bench for collectibles (See pages 67, 68, 72–74.)

(Below) Cute and silly layered animals (See pages 54–55.)

F

An example of using fun colors for country cutouts (See pages 39, 40 and 57.)

Mice with cheese and a spring bouquet of tulips (See pages 52, 53 and 76.)

These playful animal heads depict several painting options. (See pages 29 and 31.)

G

A variety of small and decorative projects (See pages 61, 130 and 147–149.)

Useful projects for the home (See pages 162, 163 and 166.)

An amusing set of mouse numbers, along with a fish sculpture (See pages 88 and 184.)

H

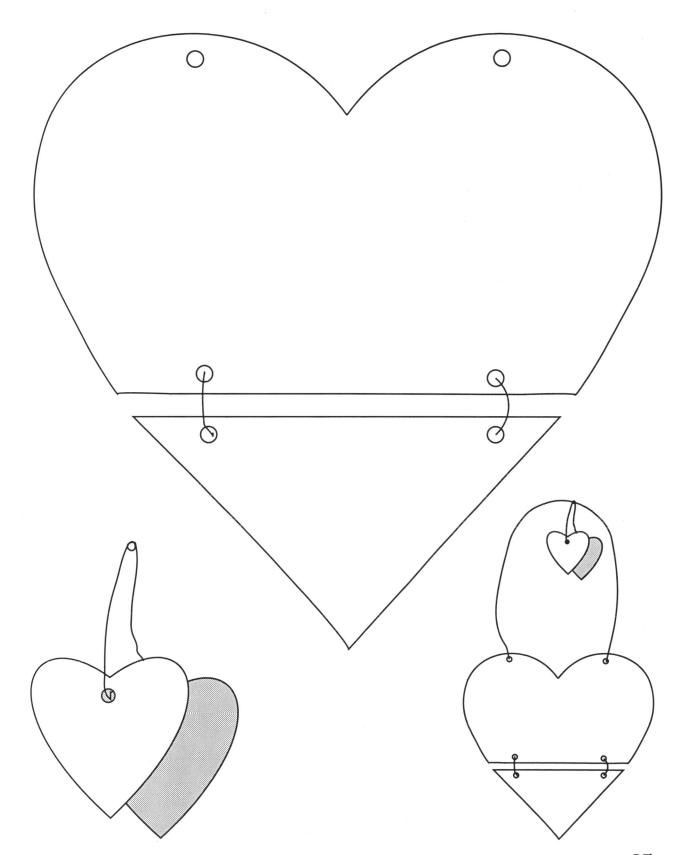

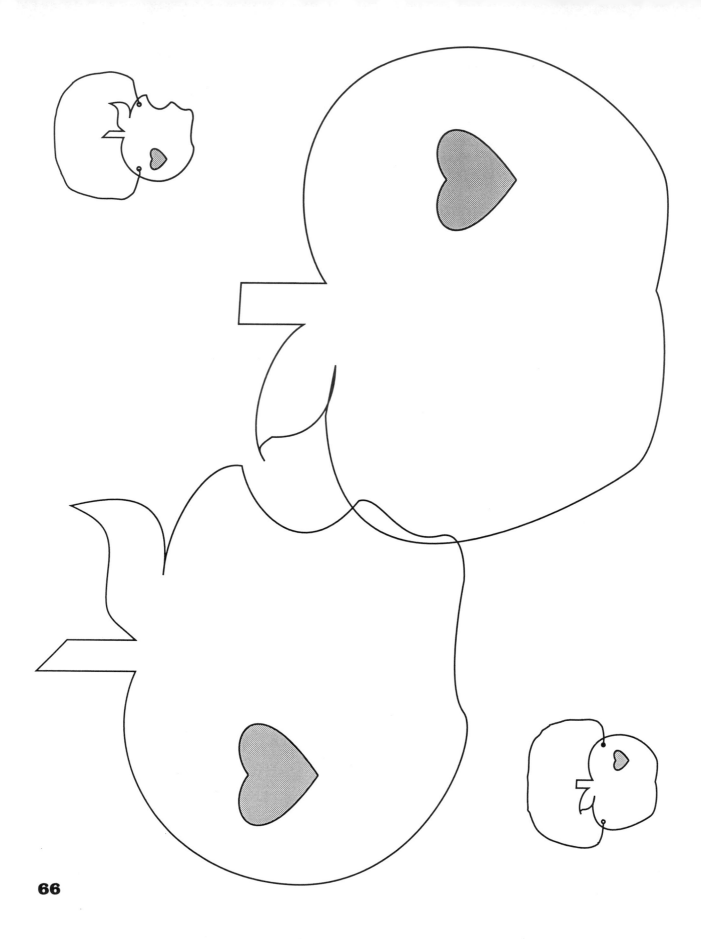

See the photo on page 69.
See page F of the color section.

Wheels are ⅞" in diameter.

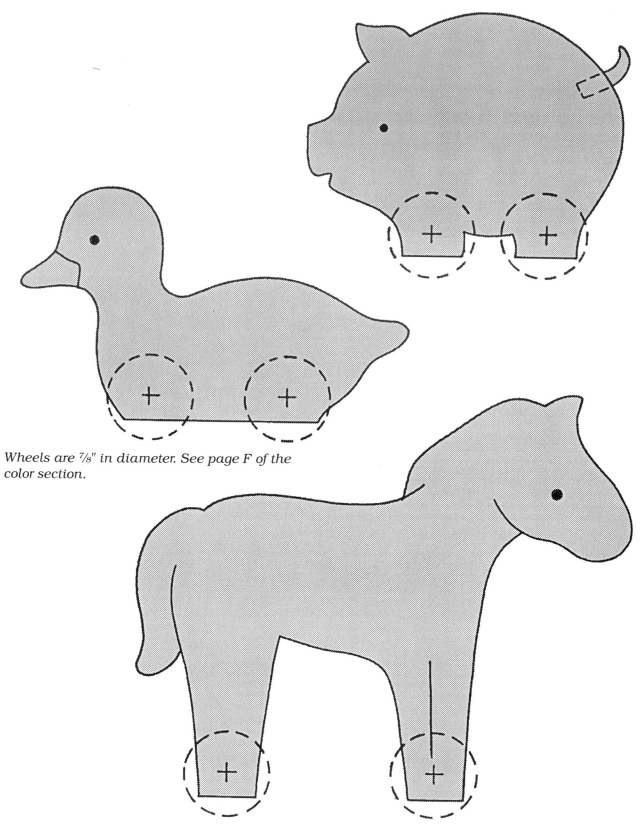

Wheels are ⅞" in diameter. See page F of the color section.

68

Wheeled animals. See page F of the color section.

Wall-hanging birdhouse with a flush back. See page C of the color section.

69

Roof material is ¼″ × 1¼″. Scalloped trim is ¼″ thick. See the photos on page 69 and page C of the color section.

BASE ¾″ x 1¾″ x 5½″

WING OVERLAYS

Bird designs. See the photos on page 69 and page C of the color section.

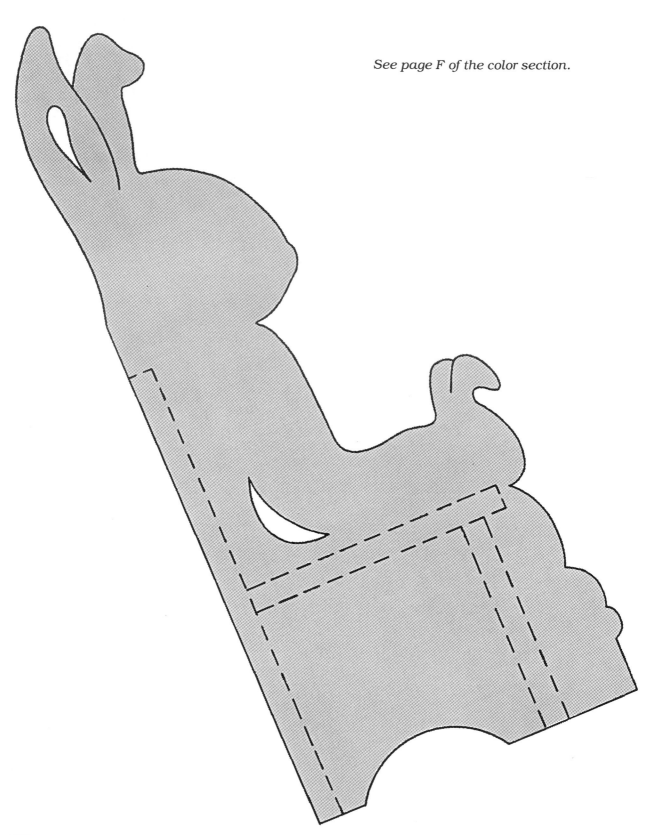

See page F of the color section.

72

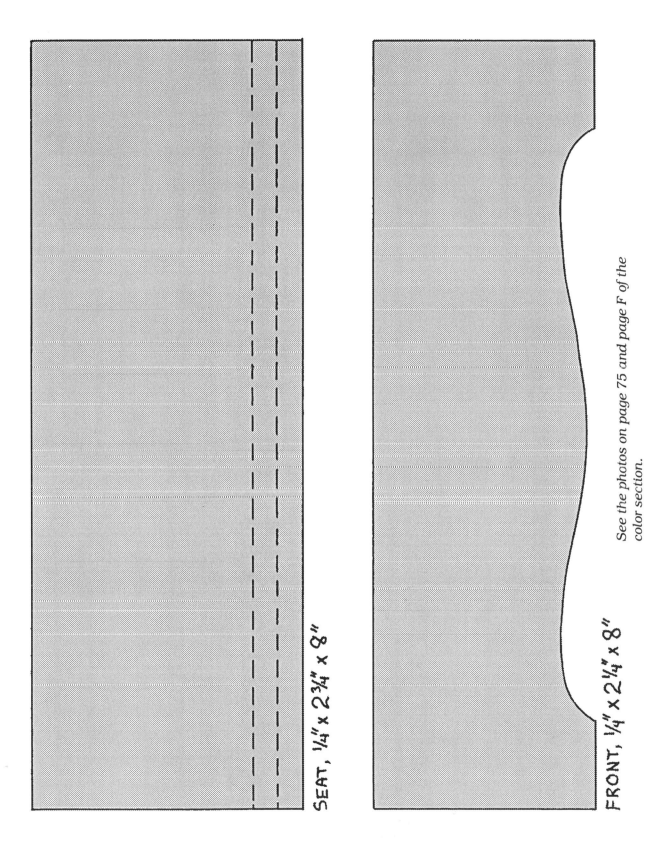

SEAT, 1/4" x 2 3/4" x 8"

FRONT, 1/4" x 2 1/4" x 8"

See the photos on page 75 and page F of the color section.

73

BACK, ¼" x 5" x 8"

See page F of the color section.

Rabbit bench, cut from ¼"-thick material. See page F of the color section.

Dimensional tulips. See page G of the color section.

See the photos on page 75 and page G of the color section.

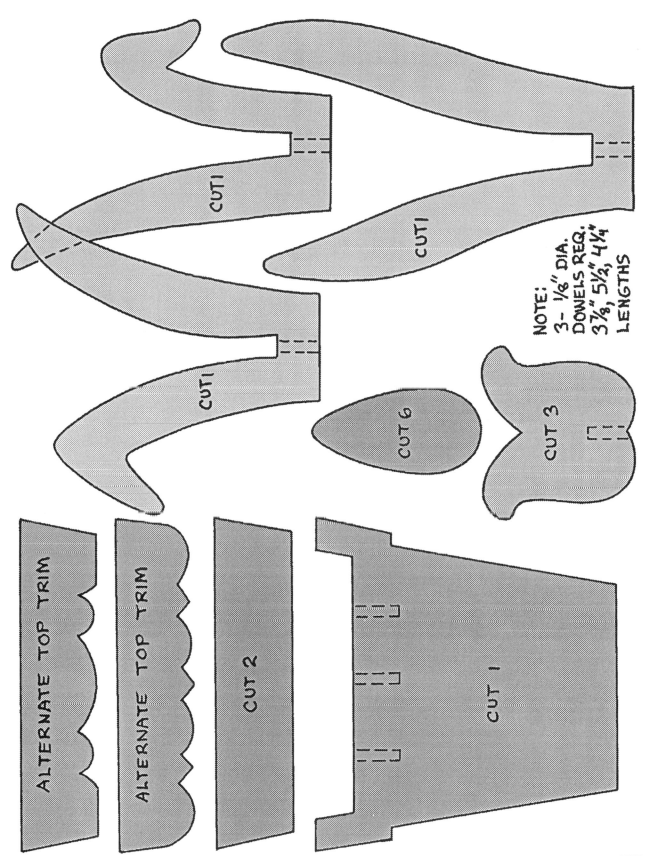

CUT 1

CUT 1

CUT 1

NOTE:
3- ⅛" DIA.
DOWELS REQ.
3⅞", 5½", 4¼"
LENGTHS

CUT 6

CUT 3

ALTERNATE TOP TRIM

ALTERNATE TOP TRIM

CUT 2

CUT 1

Weather Vanes

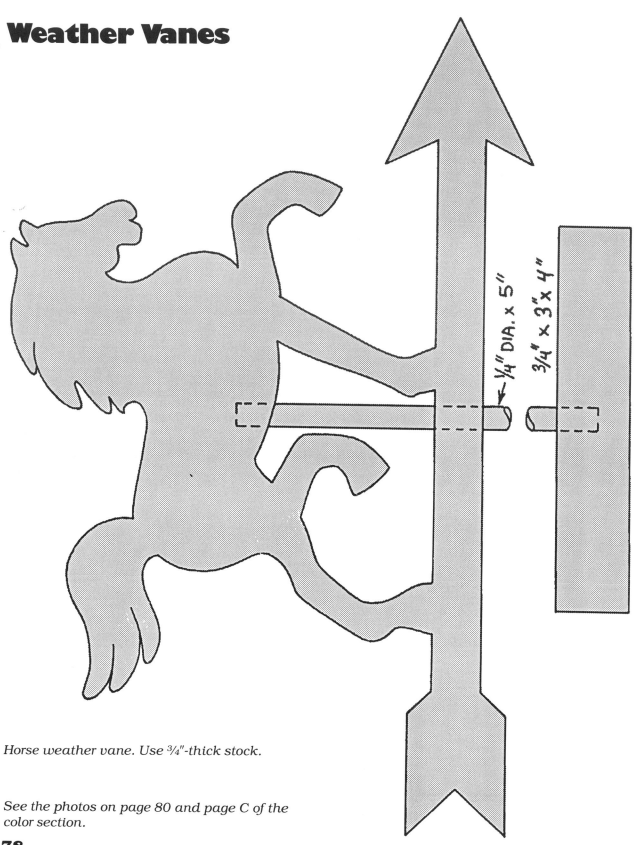

¾" DIA. x 5"

¾" x 3" x 4"

Horse weather vane. Use ¾"-thick stock.

See the photos on page 80 and page C of the color section.

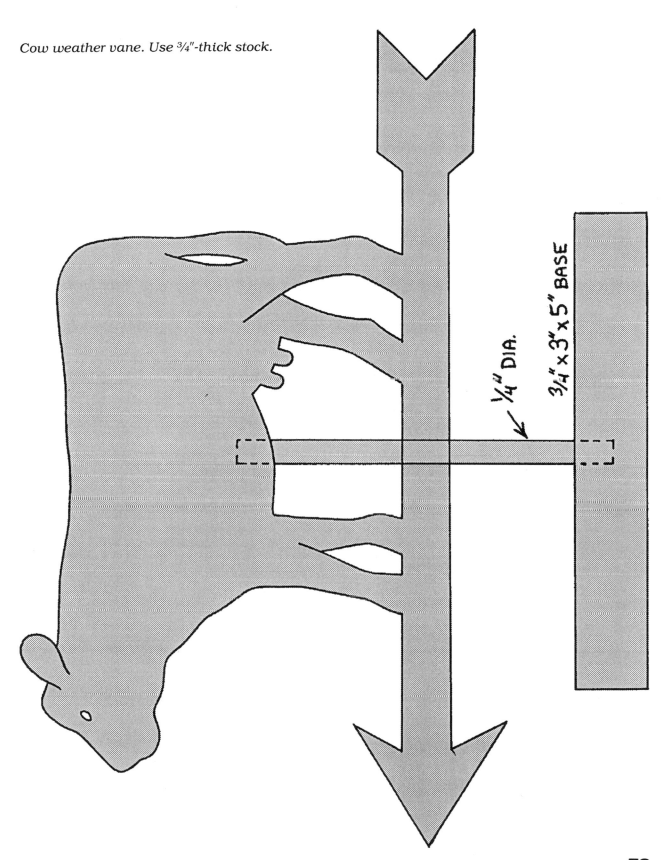

Cow weather vane. Use ¾"-thick stock.

¼" DIA.

¾" × 3" × 5" BASE

Horse weather vane. Cut from ¾"-thick material. See page C of the color section.

Rooster and hen made with ¾" stock and ½" diameter dowels. See page C of the color section.

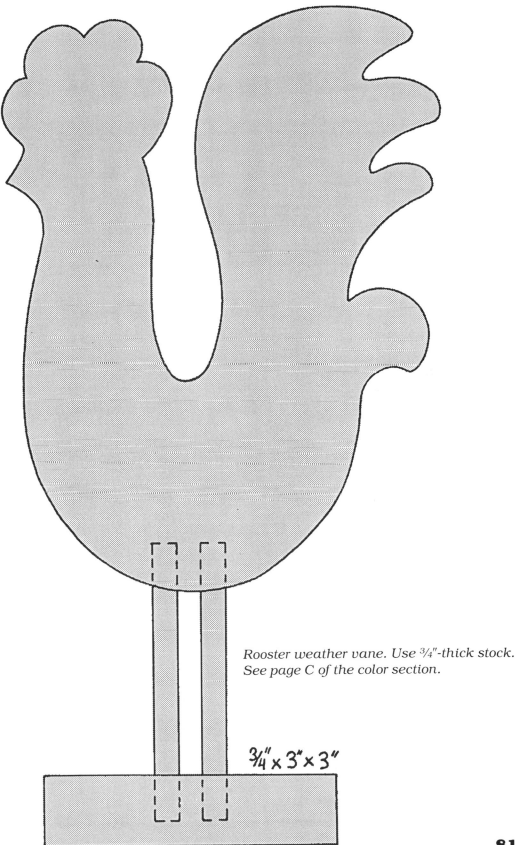

Rooster weather vane. Use ¾″-thick stock. See page C of the color section.

¾″ × 3″ × 3″

81

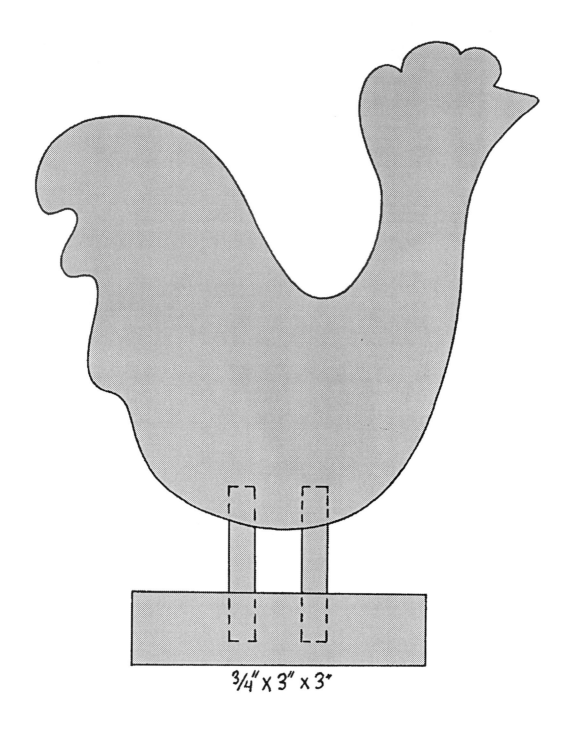

3/4" X 3" X 3"

See the photos on page 80 and page C of the color section.

1/4" DIA. X 5 1/2"

3/4" X 3" X 5" BASE

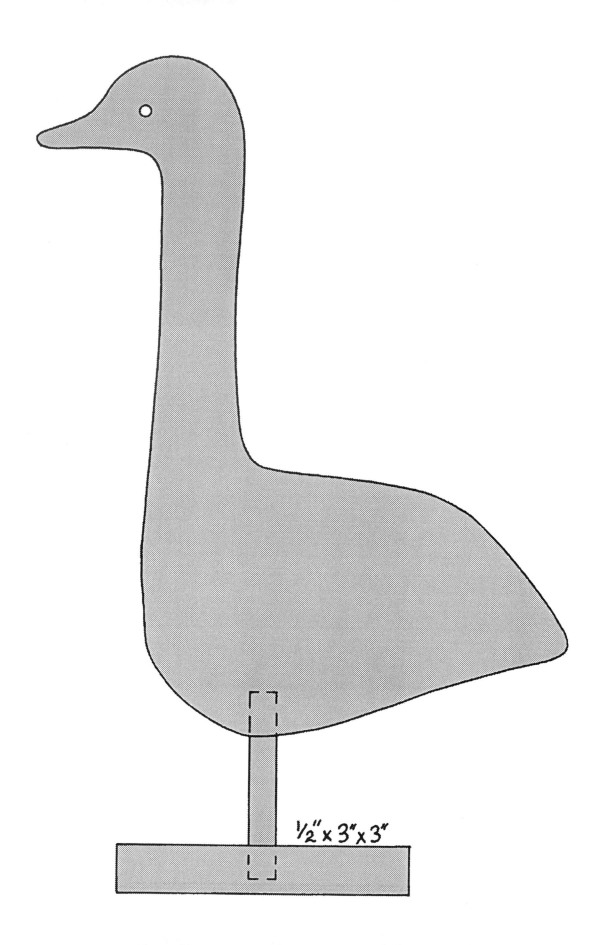

½" x 3" x 3"

$\frac{3}{4}$" x 3" x 5"

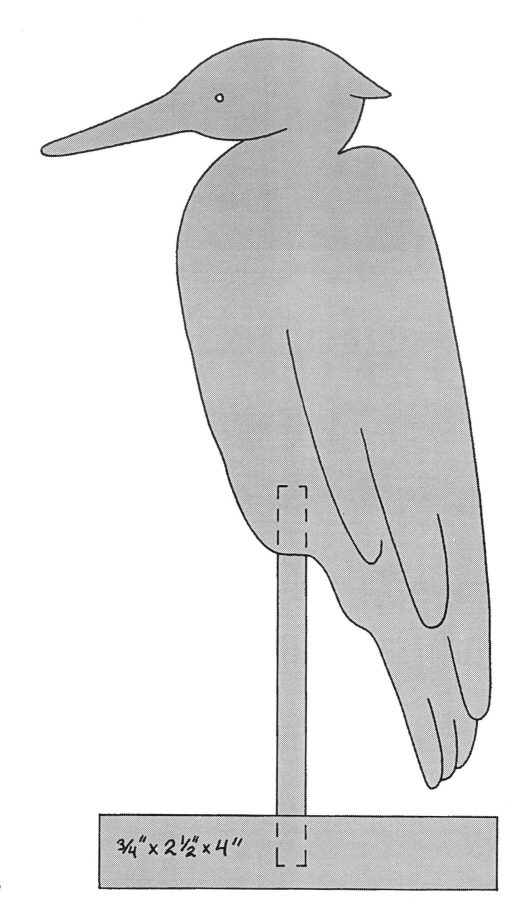

3/4" x 2 1/2" x 4"

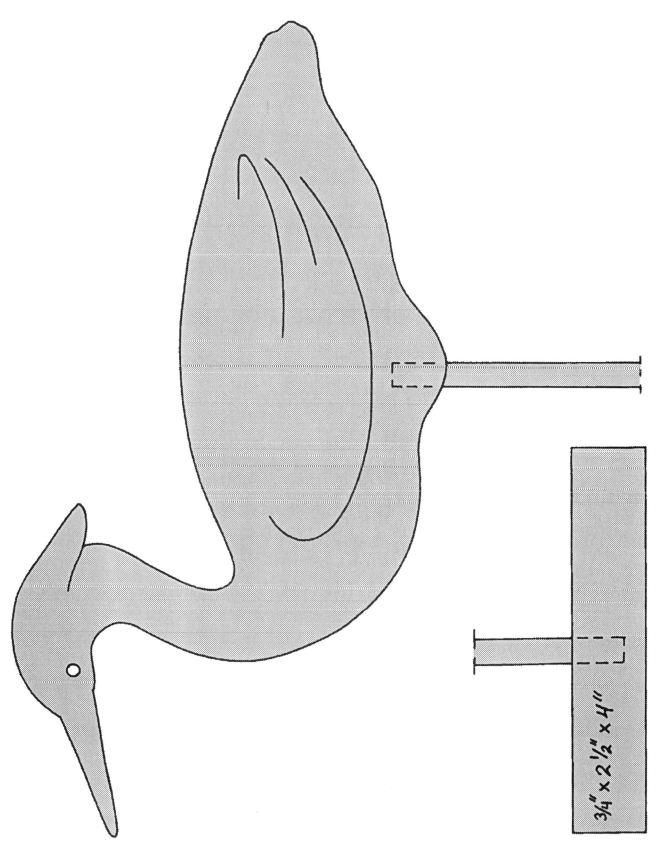

$3/4'' \times 2\frac{1}{2}'' \times 4''$

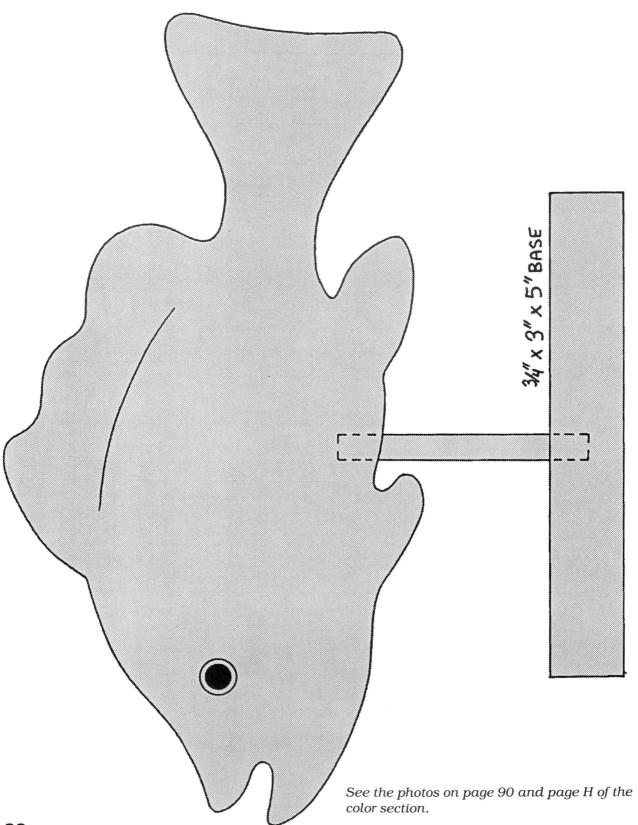

3/4" x 3" x 5" BASE

See the photos on page 90 and page H of the color section.

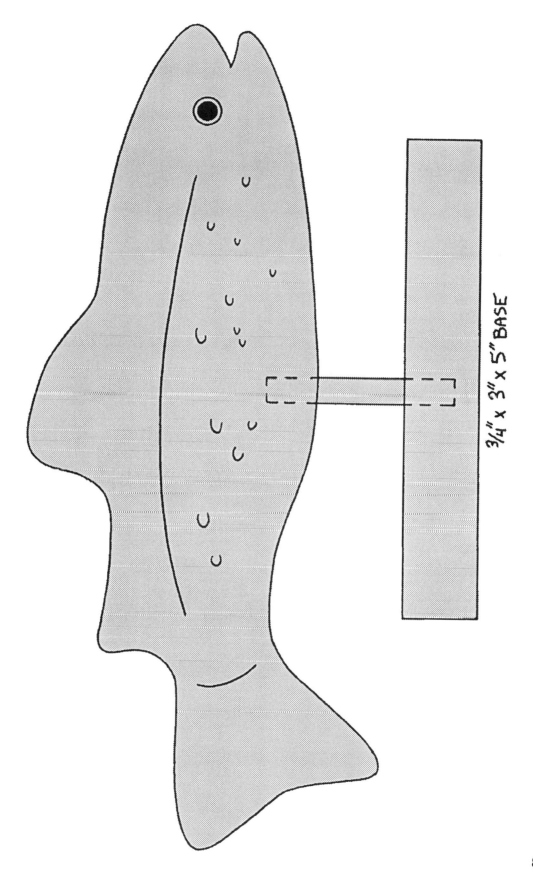

3/4″ x 3″ x 5″ BASE

89

Fish sculpture cut from ¾″-thick stock and one ¼″ diameter dowel. See page H of the color section.

Carousel horse. See page E of the color section.

Carousel horse made from ½″-thick material and one ¼″ diameter dowel. Base pieces are ½″ thick by 1″ × 3″ and 1¾″ × 4″.

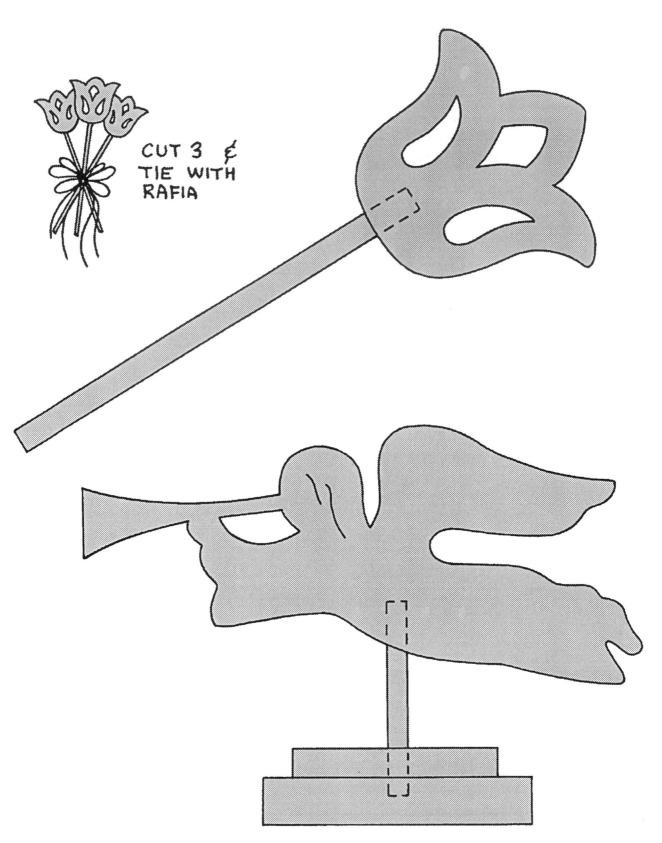

CUT 3 &
TIE WITH
RAFIA

Segmented Projects

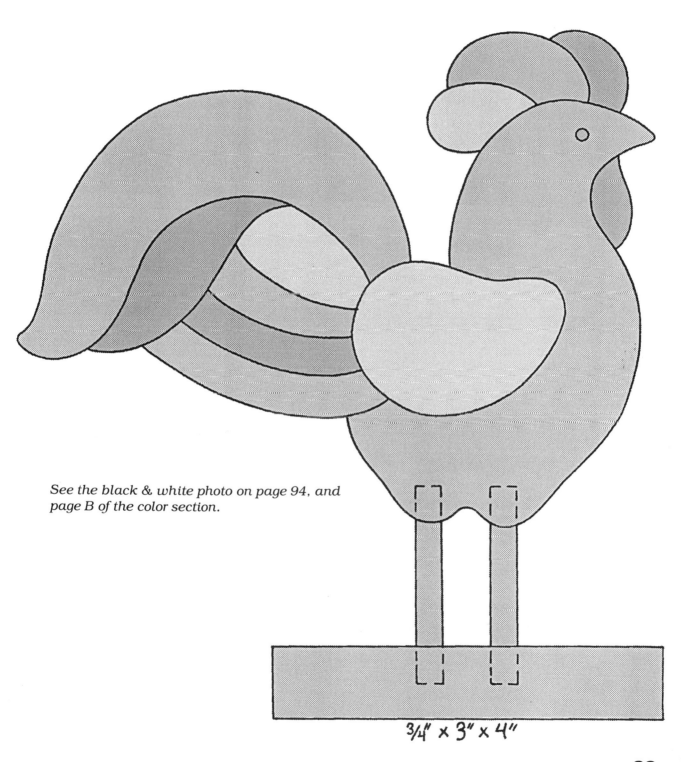

See the black & white photo on page 94, and page B of the color section.

3/4" x 3" x 4"

Segmented rooster. See page B of the color section. All segmented projects are made of ¾"-thick stock, sawn into pieces, edges rounded, pieces finished individually, and then glued back together.

A small drum sander used in a drill press speeds the rounding of segmented edges. Hand files and/or abrasives are also used.

See the photos on page 96 and page B of the color section.

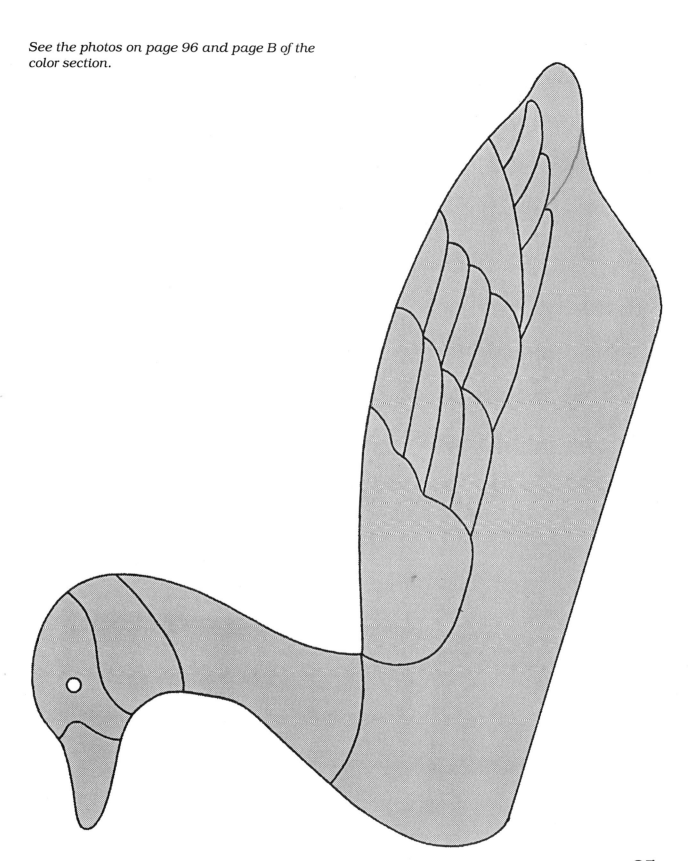

Segmented Canada goose. See page B of the color section.

*Segmented wood duck. See
page B of the color section.*

Segmented merganser. See page B of the color section.

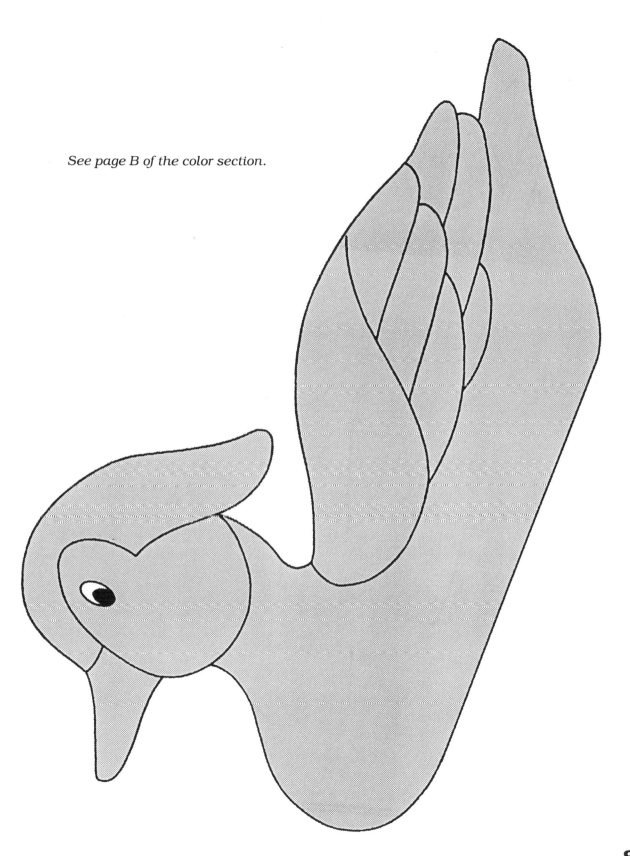

See page B of the color section.

See the photos on page 96 and page B of the color section.

OVERLAY

Welcome Signs

OVERLAYS

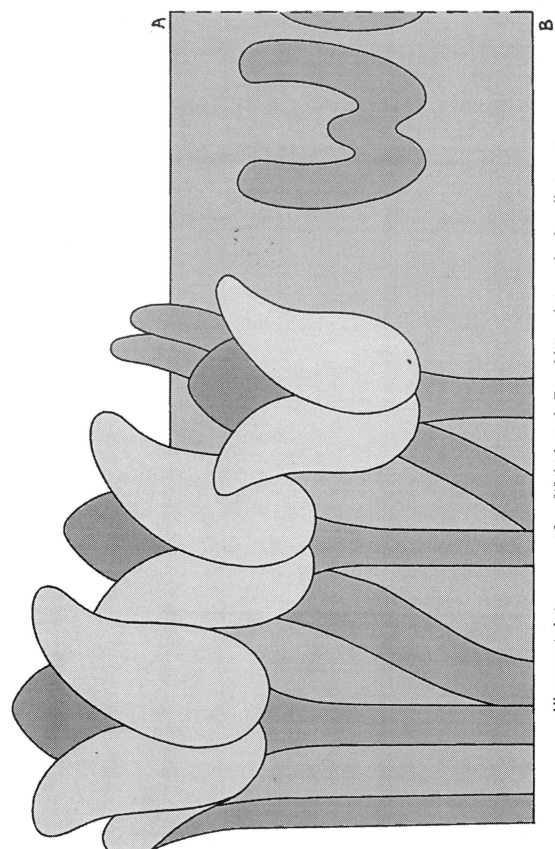

All segmented signs are cut from ¾"-thick stock. For additional strength, glue all pieces to a thin plywood backing.

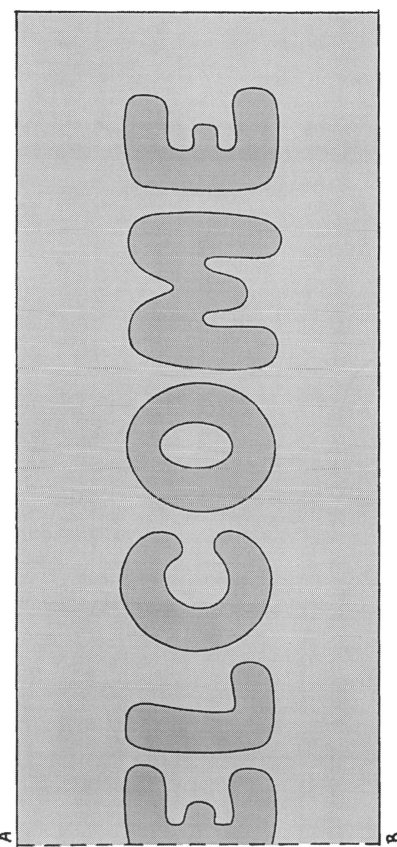

See the photos on page 104 and page B of the color section.

See the photos on page 104 and page B of the color section.

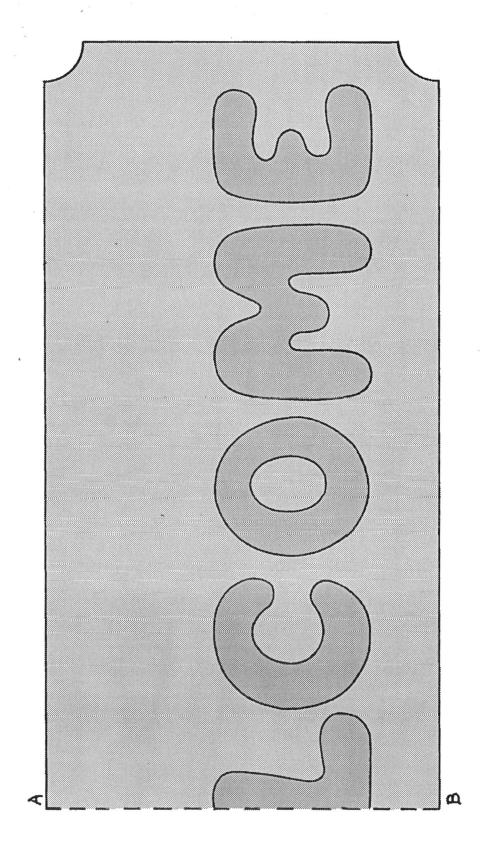

All overlay pieces are ¼" thick, glued to a backing plaque ½" to ¾" thick.

Welcome signs with segmented and round-over detailing. See page B of the color section.

A small round-over bit in a Dremel tool that's mounted in a router base accessory makes quick work of minor round-over jobs.

Use a small round file to round over the edges of small inside curves.

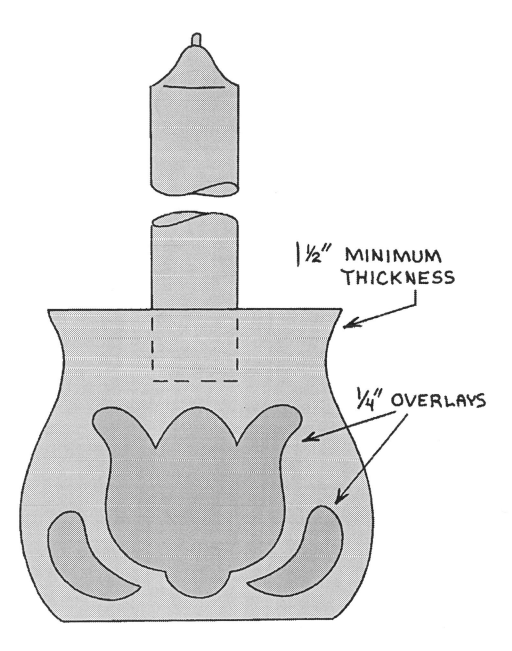

1½" MINIMUM THICKNESS

¼" OVERLAYS

See the photo on page 107.

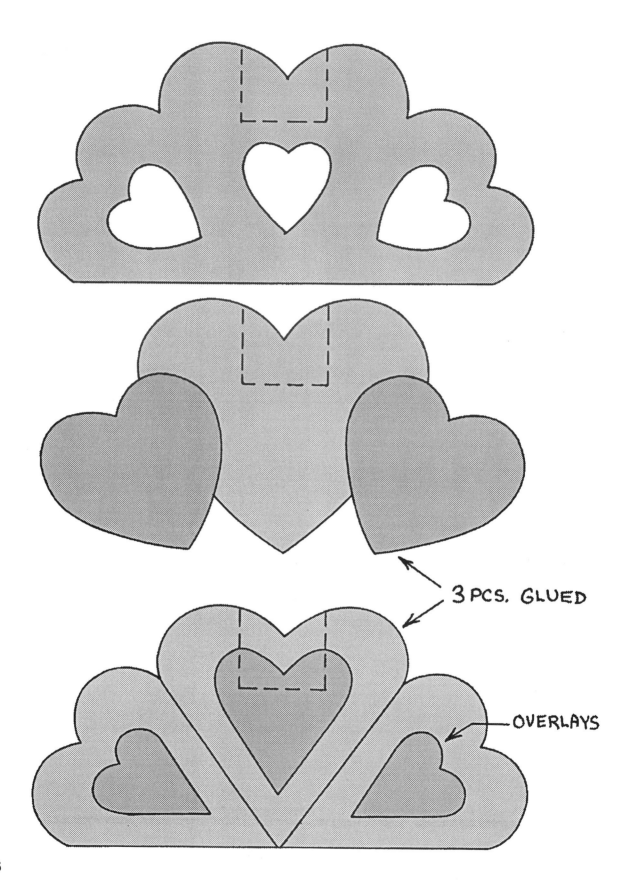

3 PCS. GLUED

OVERLAYS

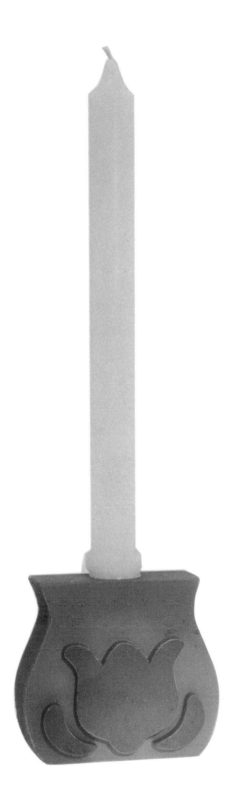

Two-piece candle holder of ½"-thick material, assembled with a slip joint. This project can be taken apart for easy storage.

Candle holder. The overlay piece could also be pierced.

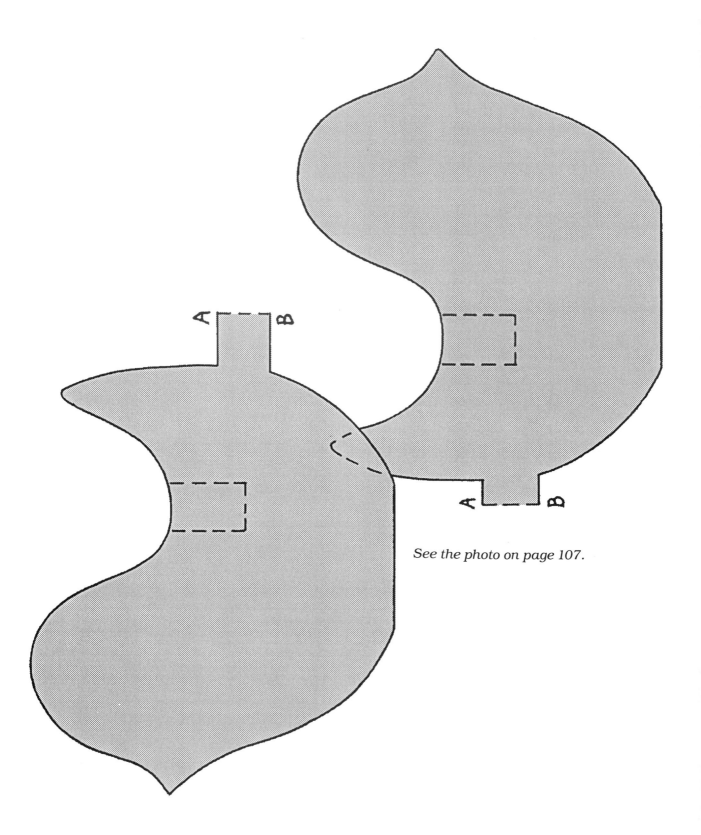

A

B

A

B

See the photo on page 107.

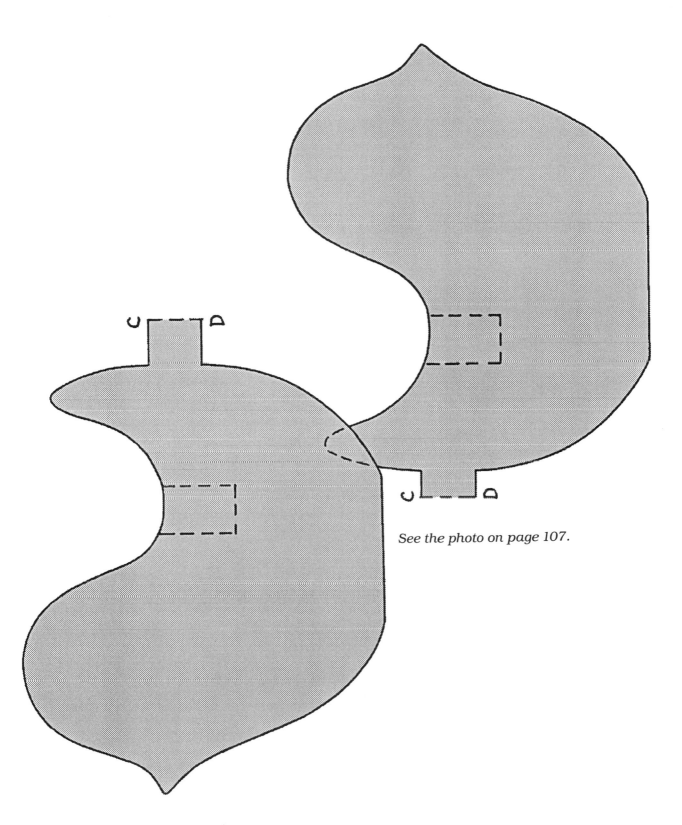

C ⌐ ⌐ D

See the photo on page 107.

C ⌐ ⌐ D

109

Kitchen Projects

See the photos on page 112 and page B of the color section.

B

A

B

A

Use fine-grain hardwood, ½" or thicker, paint the design on one side, leave the other side plain for a cutting surface.

111

Sunflower cutting board and letter/napkin holder. See page B of the color section.

Paper-towel holder. See page 137 for a matching duck shelf with pegs and page B of the color section.

112

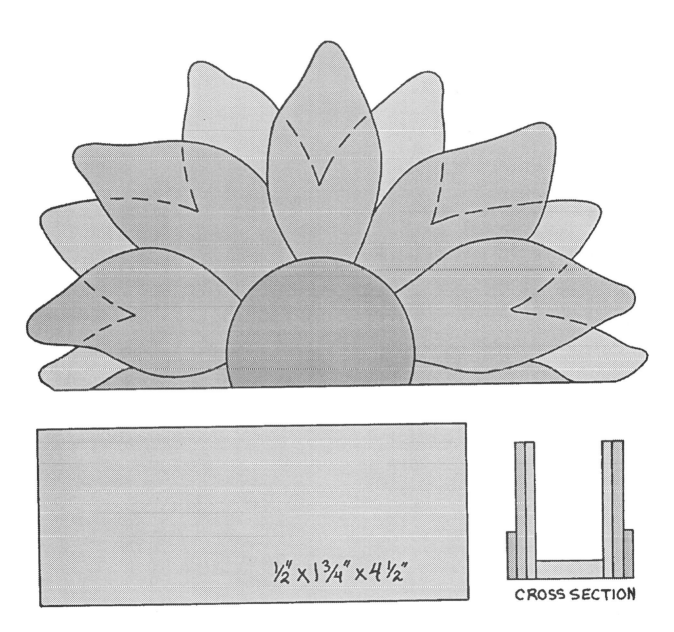

½" X 1¾" X 4½"

CROSS SECTION

Cut sunflower components of ¼"-thick material. See page B of the color section.

113

BASE
½" x 2" x 2 ¾"

Apple napkin holder. Stack two pieces from ¼"-thick material. See page 136 for a matching cup-rack project and page B of the color section.

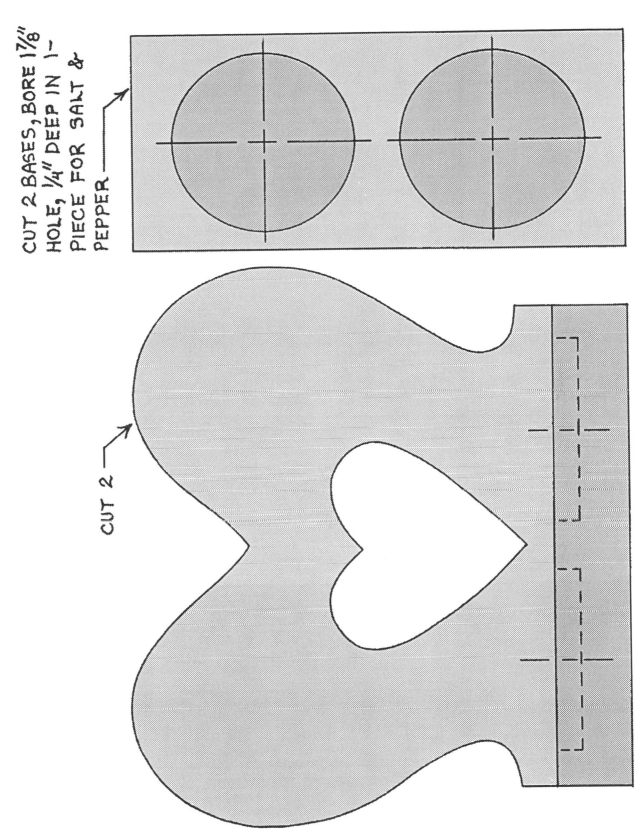

CUT 2 BASES, BORE 1⅞"
HOLE, ¼" DEEP IN 1-
PIECE FOR SALT &
PEPPER

CUT 2 →

Combination napkin, salt and pepper holder. See page 133 for a matching
pegboard/cup rack and page B of the color section.

115

Apple cutting board. Enlarge as desired.

116

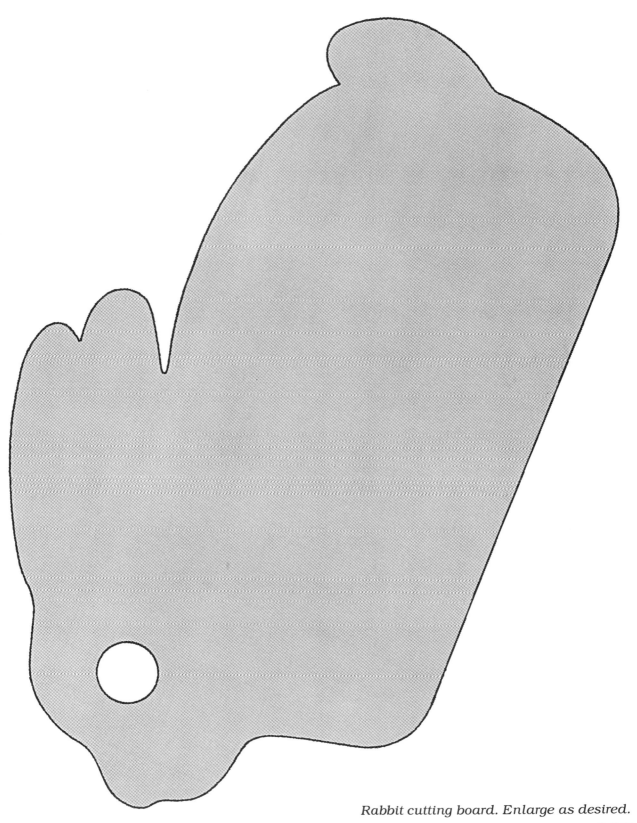

Rabbit cutting board. Enlarge as desired.

117

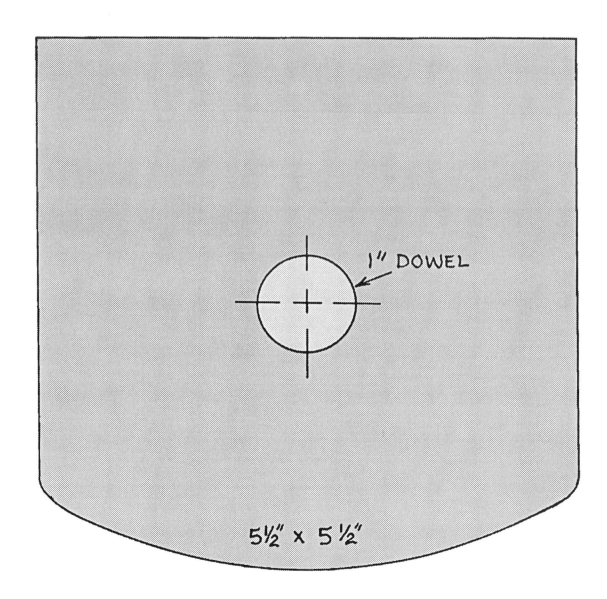

1" DOWEL

5½" x 5½"

Duck towel rack. Use all ¾"-thick stock and a 1" diameter dowel, 10" long. See the photos on page 112 and page B of the color section.

A   B

A   B

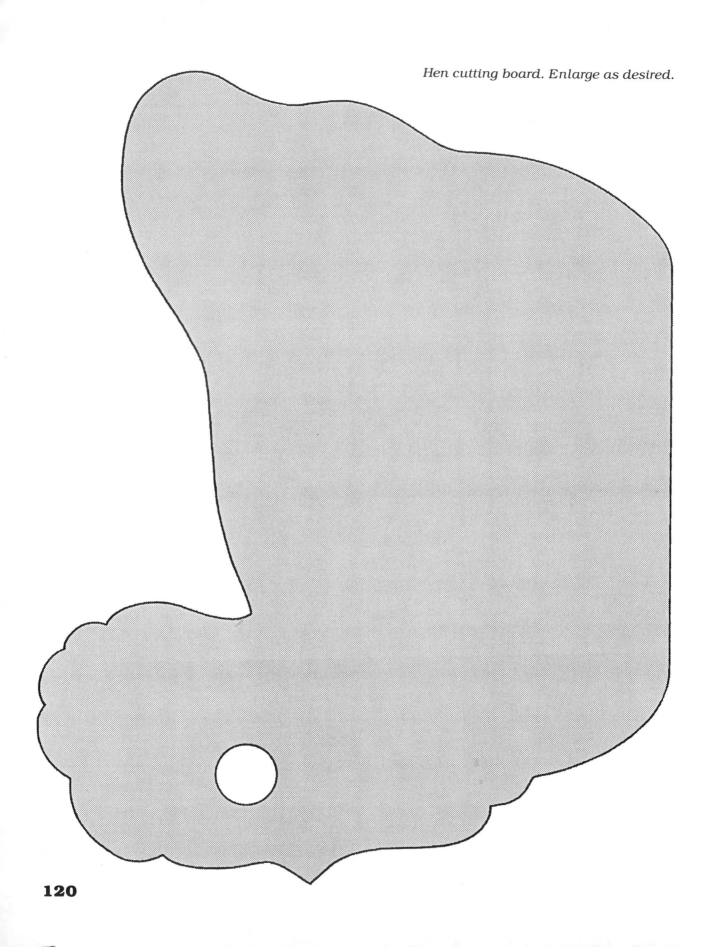

Hen cutting board. Enlarge as desired.

120

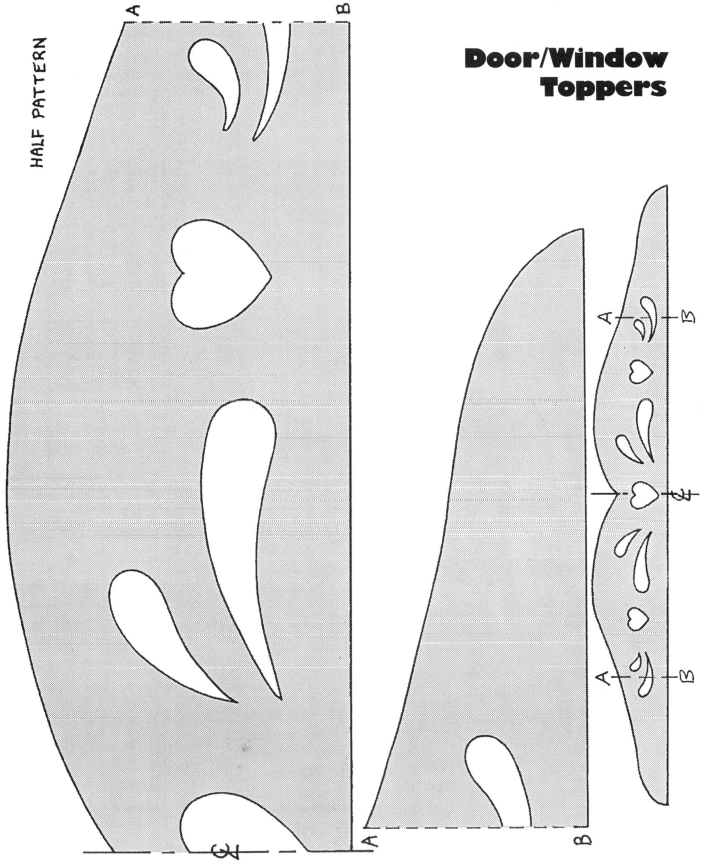

Door/Window
Toppers

HALF PATTERN

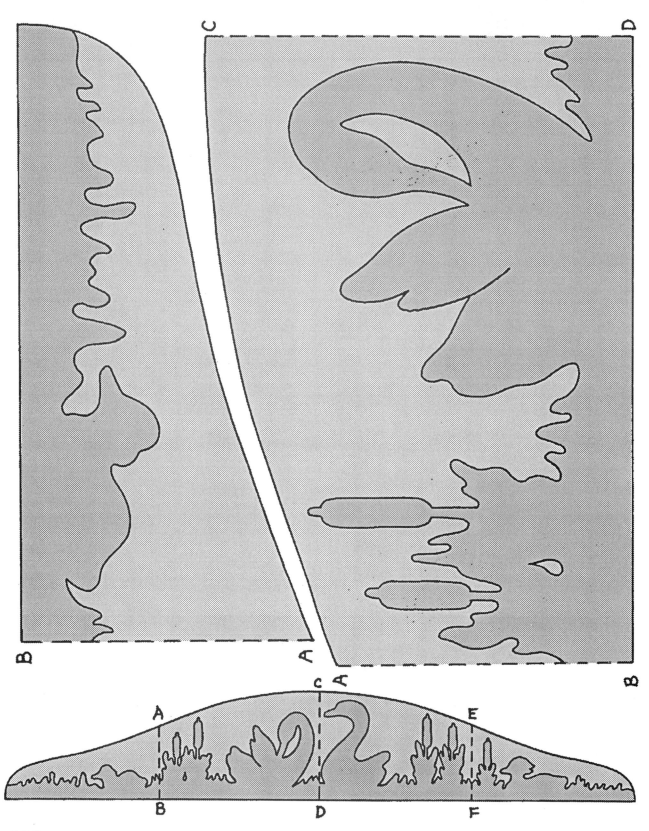

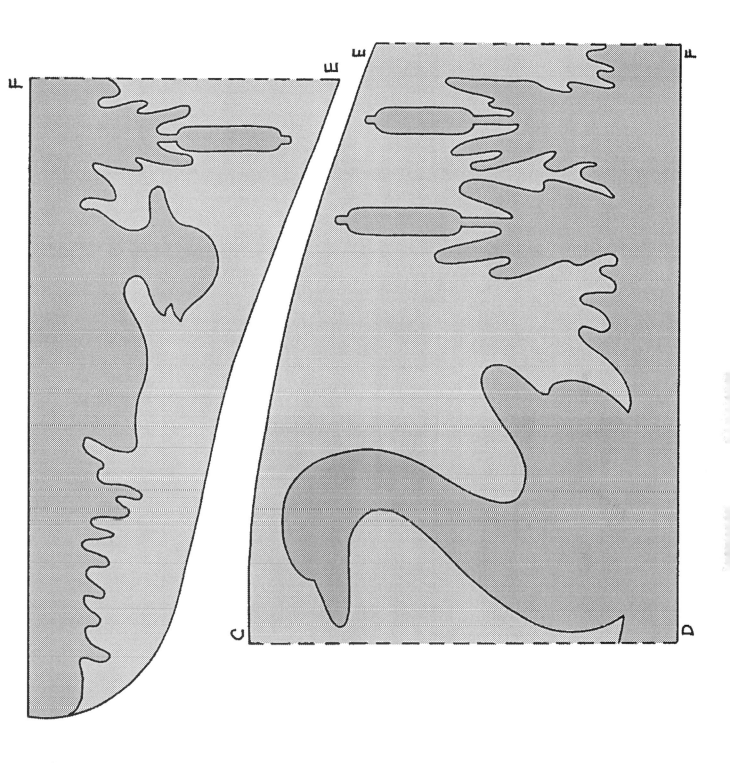

See the photos on page 128 and page E of the color section.

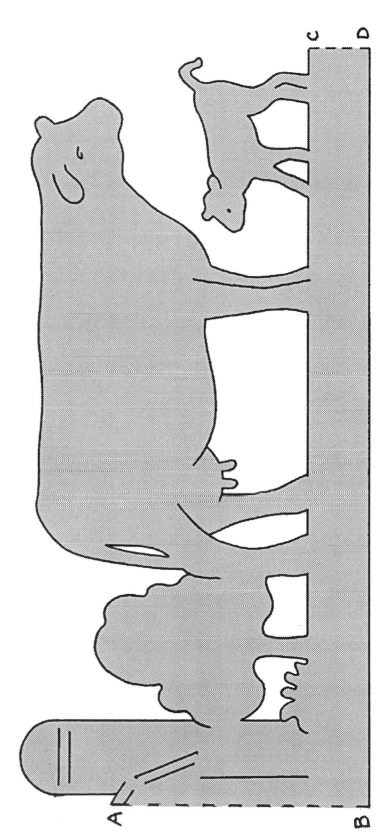

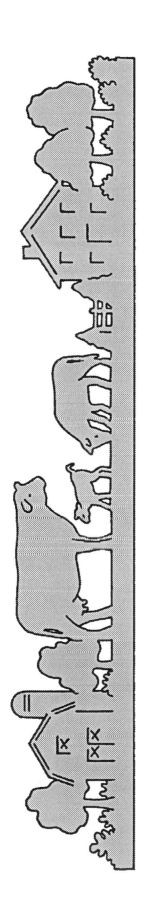

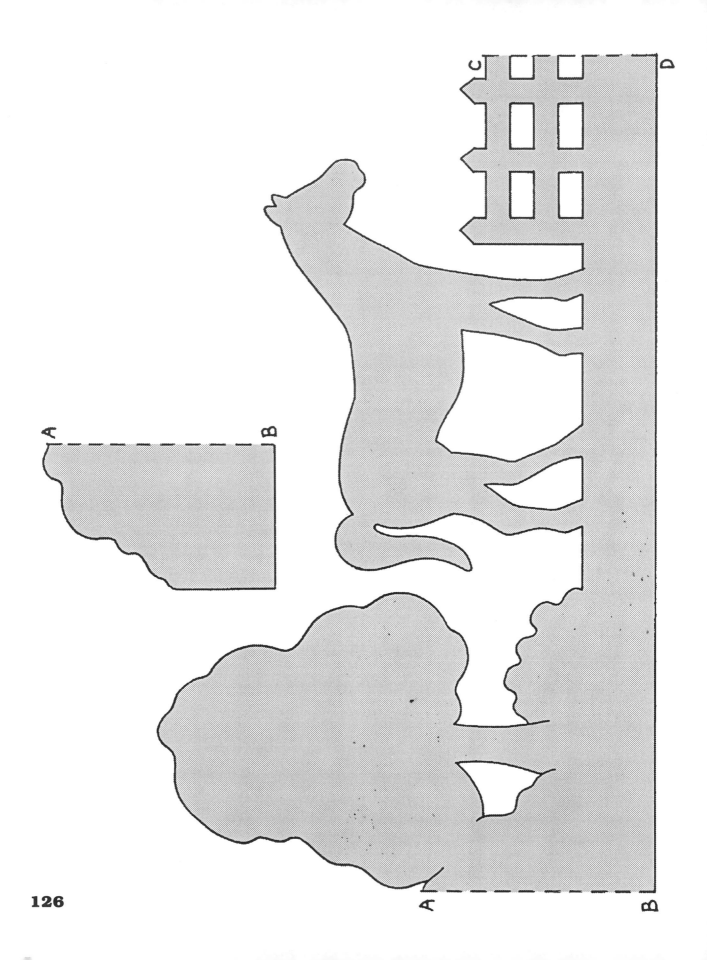

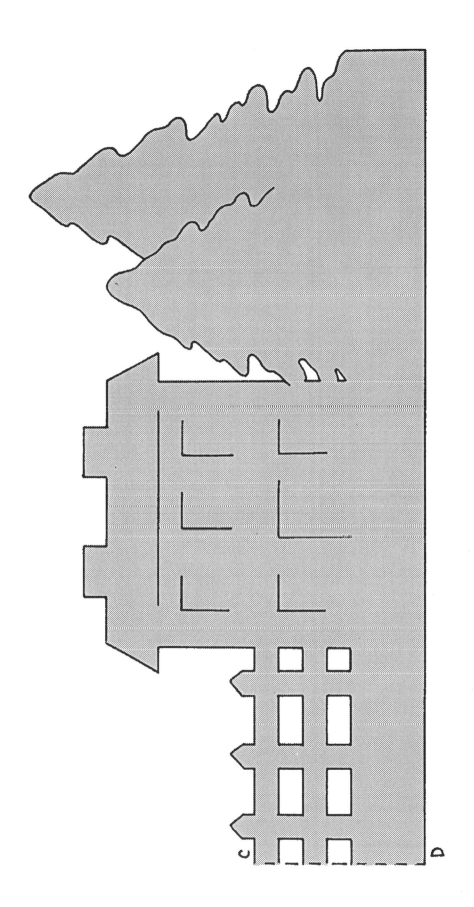

C

D

127

Door/window topper above is made of a ¾"-thick solid-wood back and ¼" overlay material. The design alone makes an interesting silhouette. See page E of the color section.

This shelf cat can be converted to a key or jewelry rack with the addition of "L" hooks or small wooden pegs. See the pattern and page D of the color section.

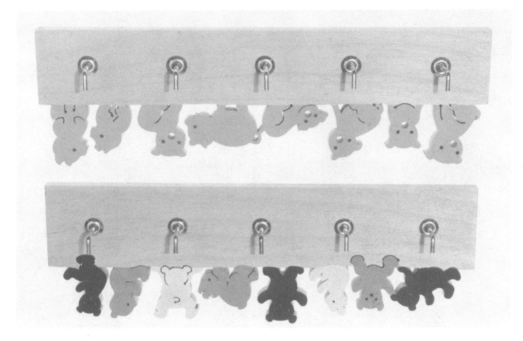

Small racks can take on a different look and
a different use by substituting small wooden
pegs. See page H of the color section.

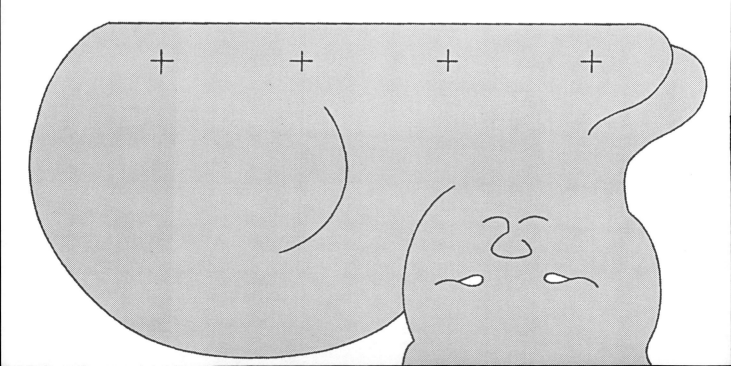

See the photos on page 129 and page H of the color section.

ALTERNATE DESIGN

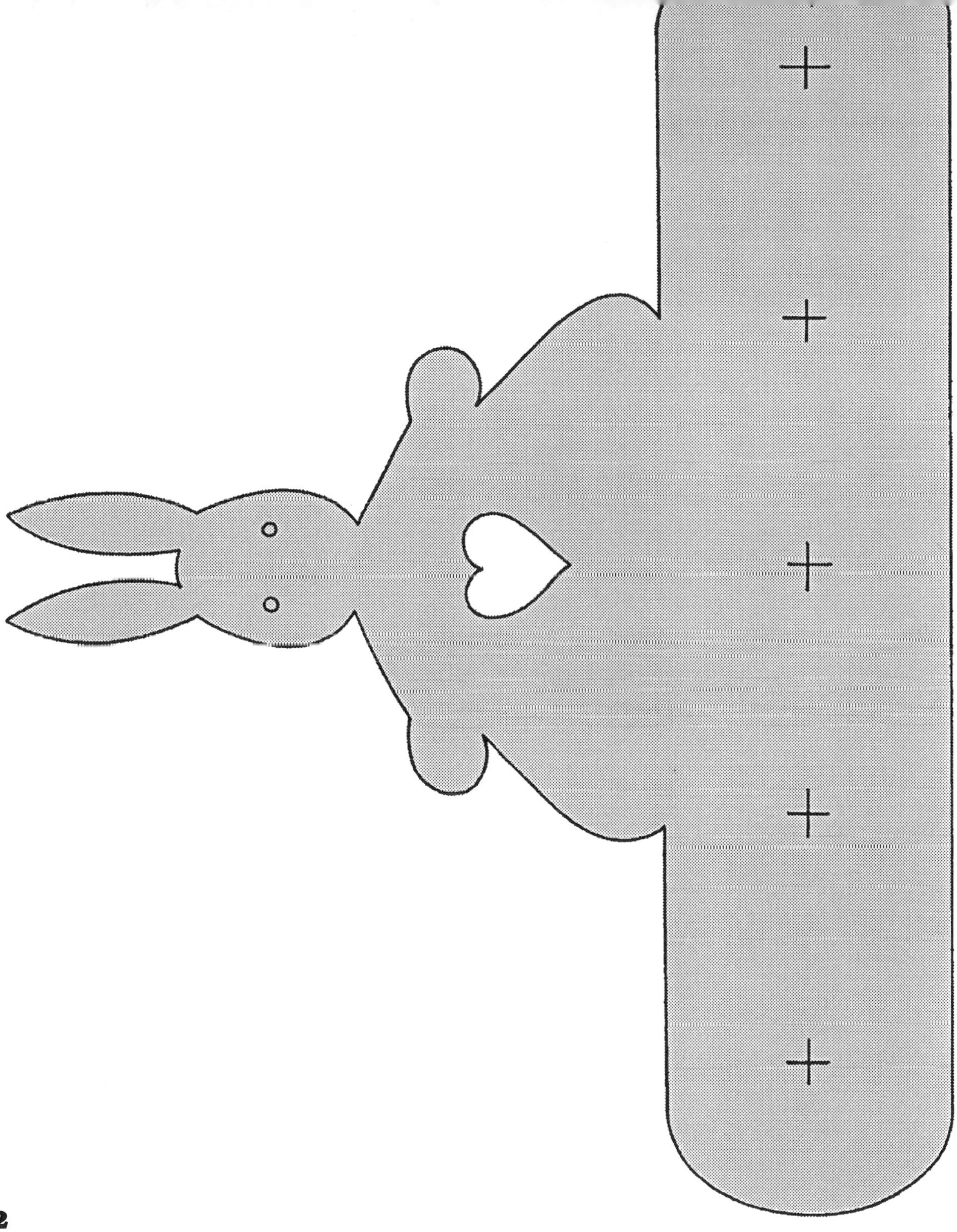

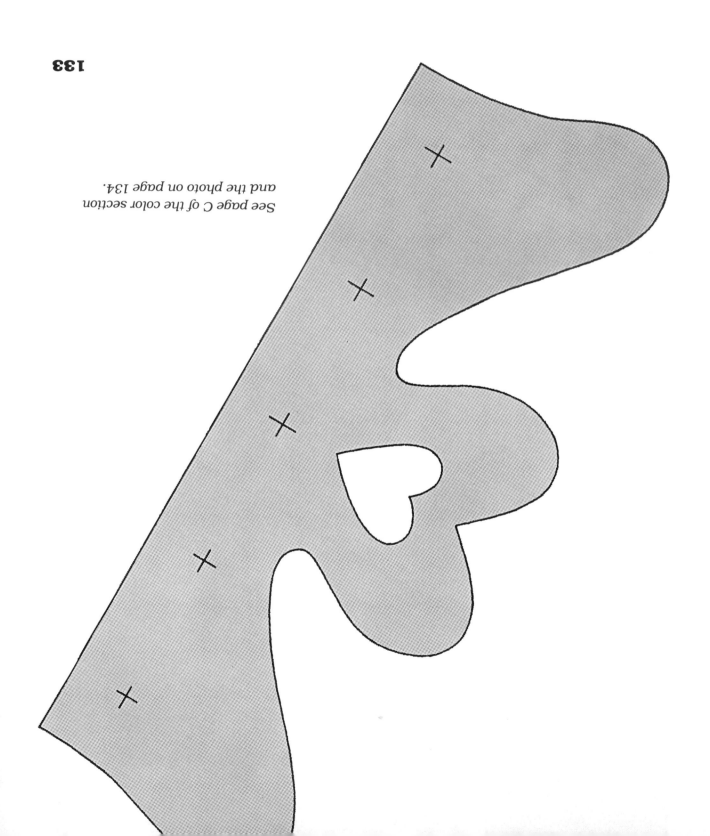

See page C of the color section and the photo on page 134.

Matching set. The pegboards have various uses. See pages B and C of the color section.

Apple designs. See pages B and C of the color section.

134

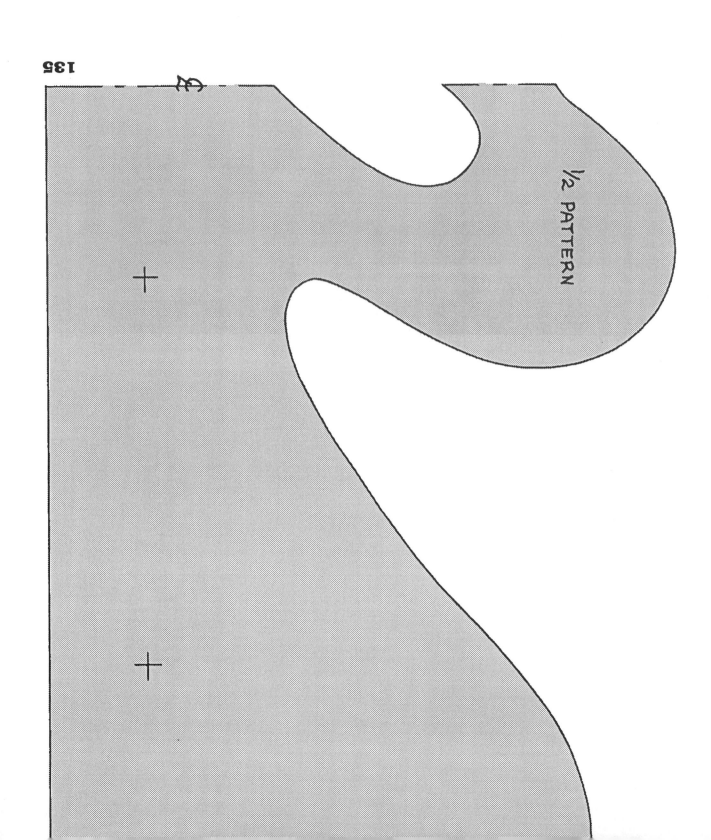

135

½ PATTERN

OVERLAPPING PATTERN

This pattern can be used as a single pegboard or continued to any length by overlapping, as shown. See the photos on page 134 and page C of the color section.

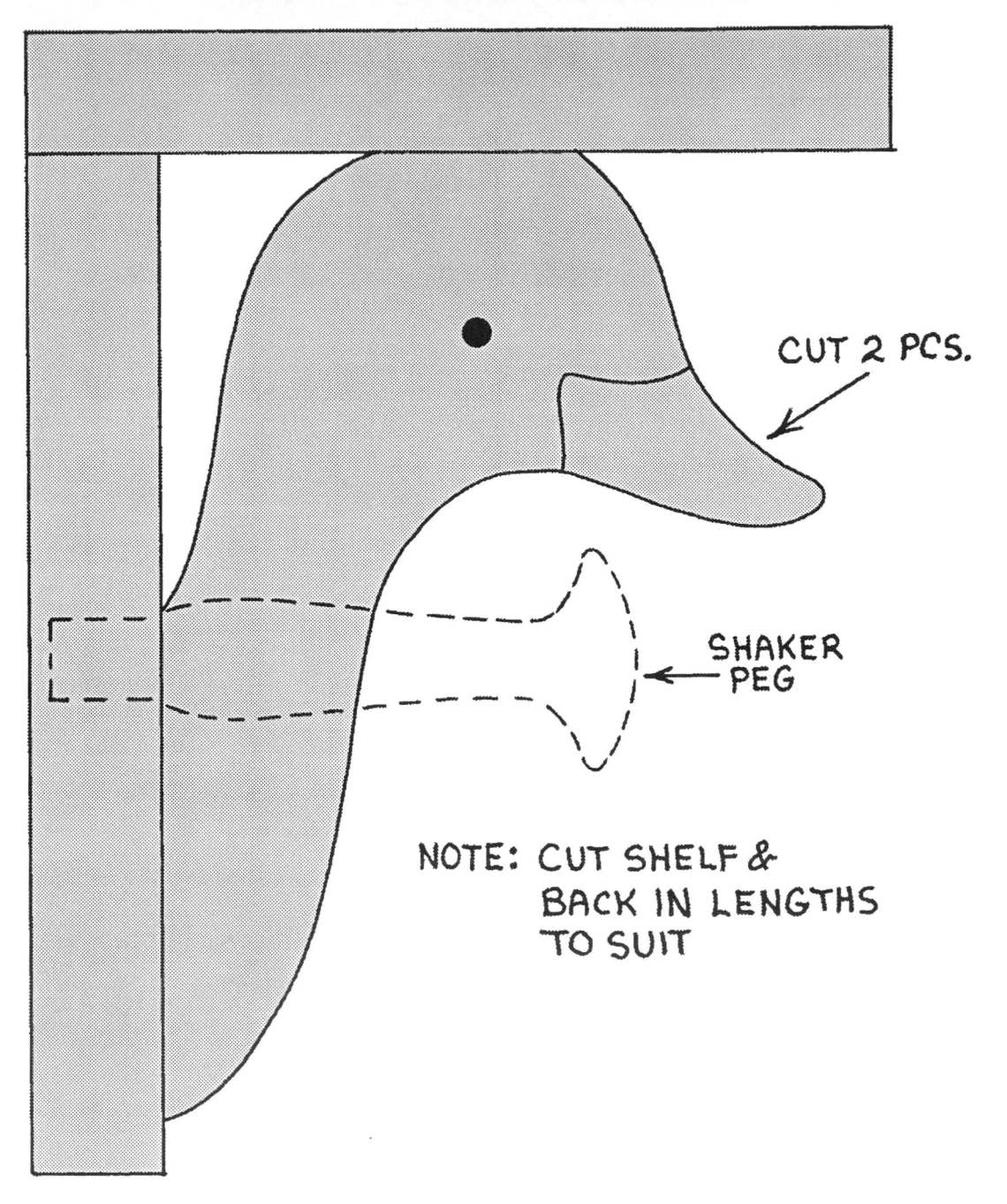

CUT 2 PCS.

SHAKER PEG

NOTE: CUT SHELF &
BACK IN LENGTHS
TO SUIT

See the photos on page 141 and page D of the color section.

137

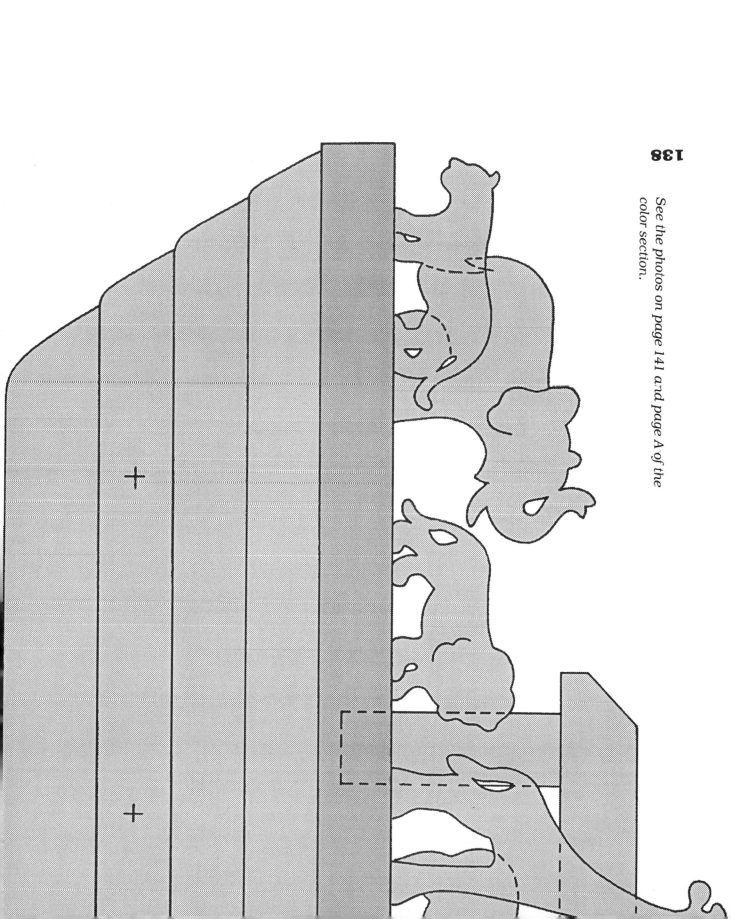

See the photos on page 141 and page A of the color section.

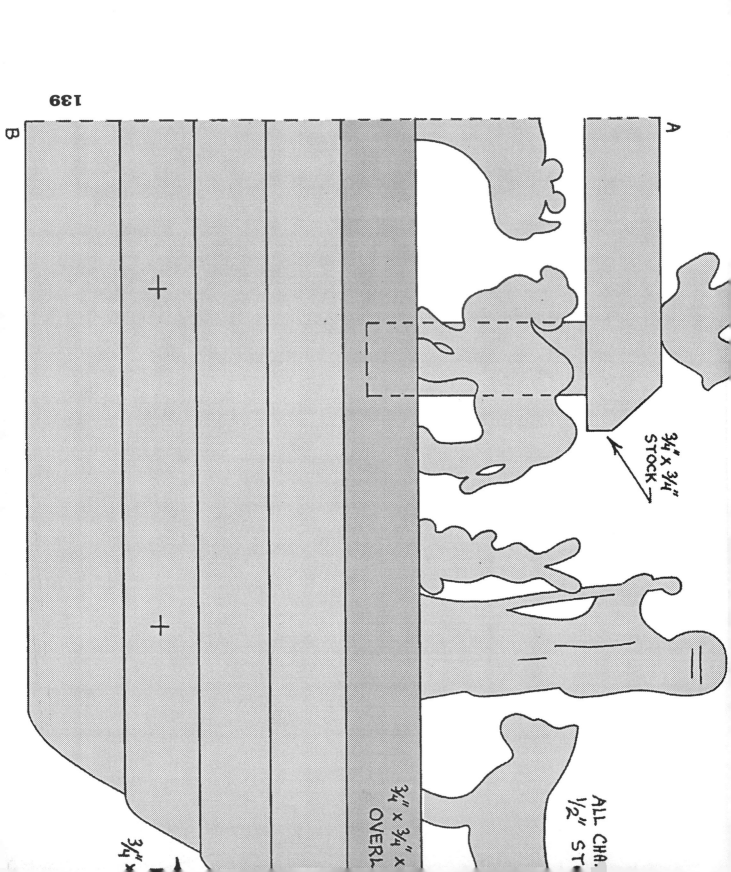

139

Animal patterns for the Noah's Ark coat rack. See page A of the color section.

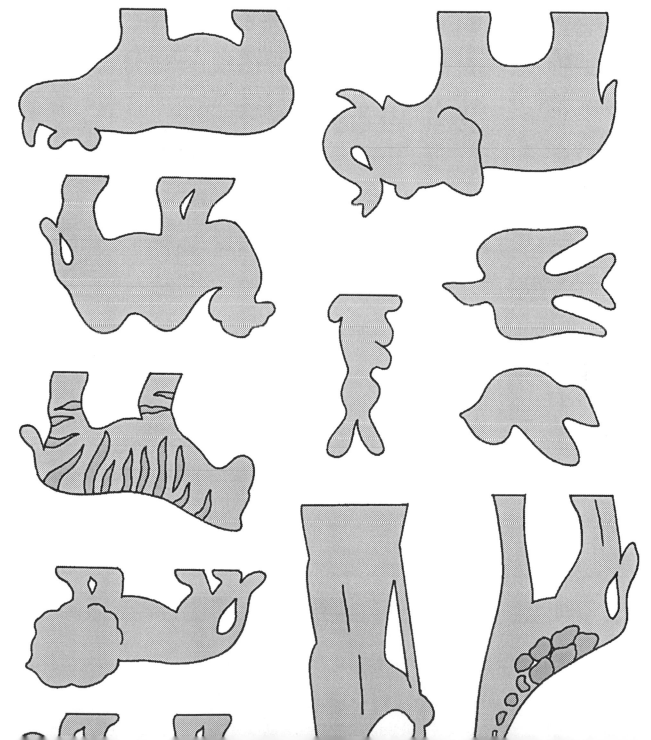

Noah's Ark coat rack. See page A of the color section.

Pegboard design that can also be used as a silhouette door/window topper. See page E of the color section.

Duck shelf and pegboard. The length of the shelf and the number of pegs can be varied. See page D of the color section.

141

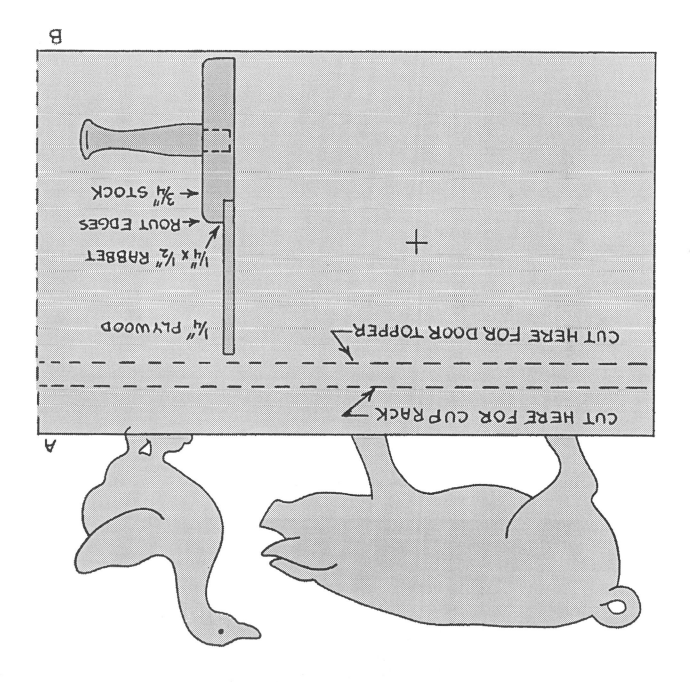

Note the reduced drawing of the side-view construction details. See the photos on page 141 and page E of the color section.

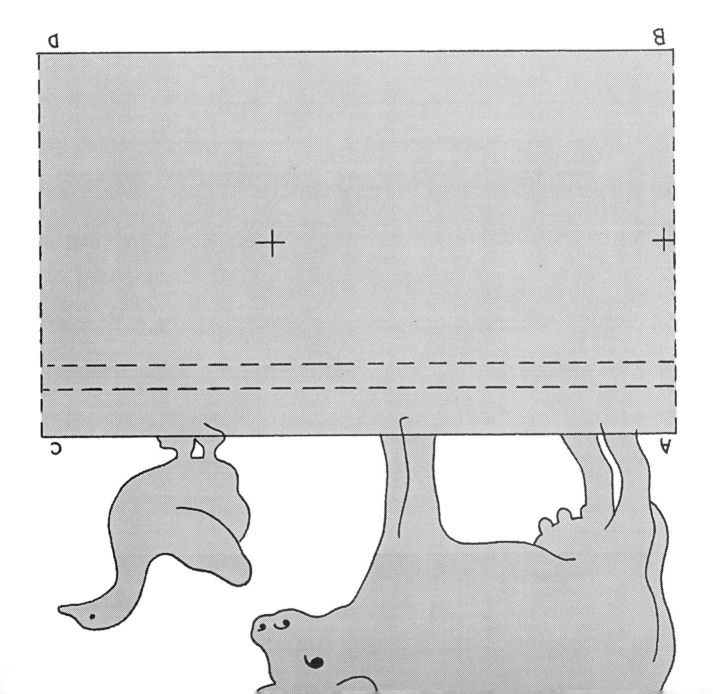

See the photos on page 141 and page E of the color section.

143

See the photos on page 141 and page E of the color section.

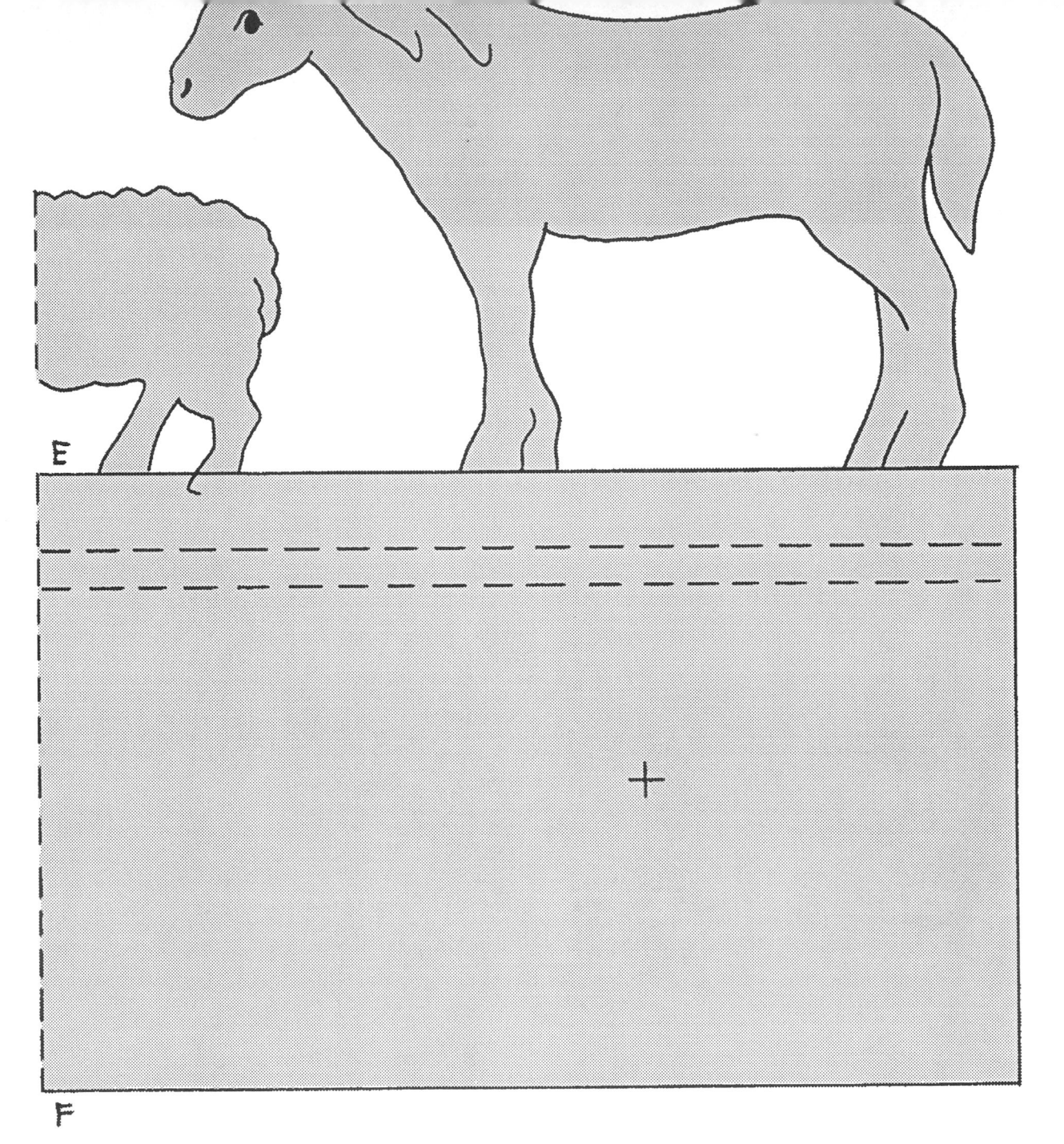

See the photos on page 141 and page E of the color section.

A shelf for miniatures. All parts are ¼" thick. See page H of the color section.

146

Miniature-collection box. See page D of the color section.

SHELF, CUT 4
1/4" X 1" X 15/8"

A

B

B

A

See page H of the color section.

See the photos on page 146 and pages C, D
and H of the color section.

*See the photos on page 146 and pages D and
H of the color section.*

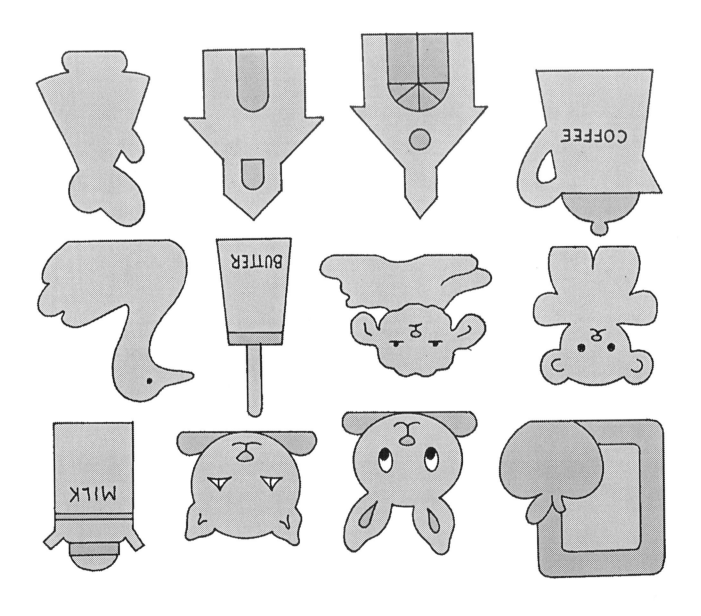

All stock is ¼″ × 1½″ wide with ¼″-thick trim overlay and an optional ⅛″- to ¼″-thick plywood back. See page D of the color section.

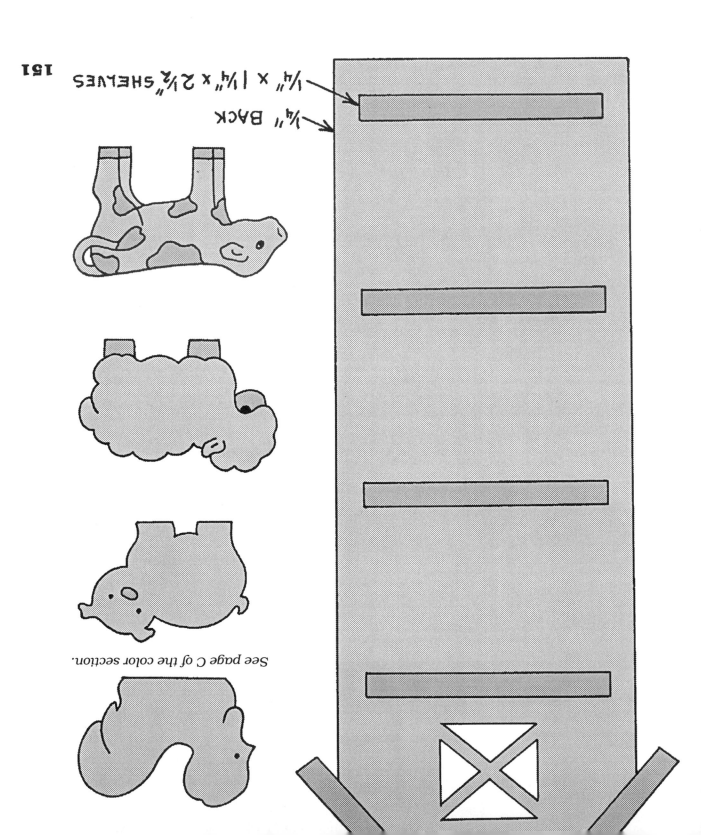

¼" × 1⅛" × 2½" SHELVES

¾" BACK

See page C of the color section.

151

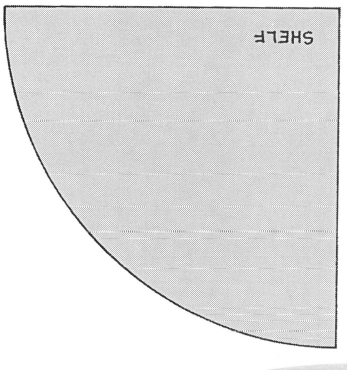

SHELF

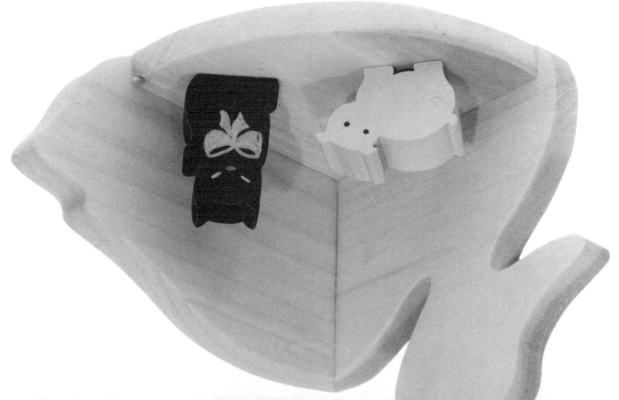

45° ANGLE CUTS

B

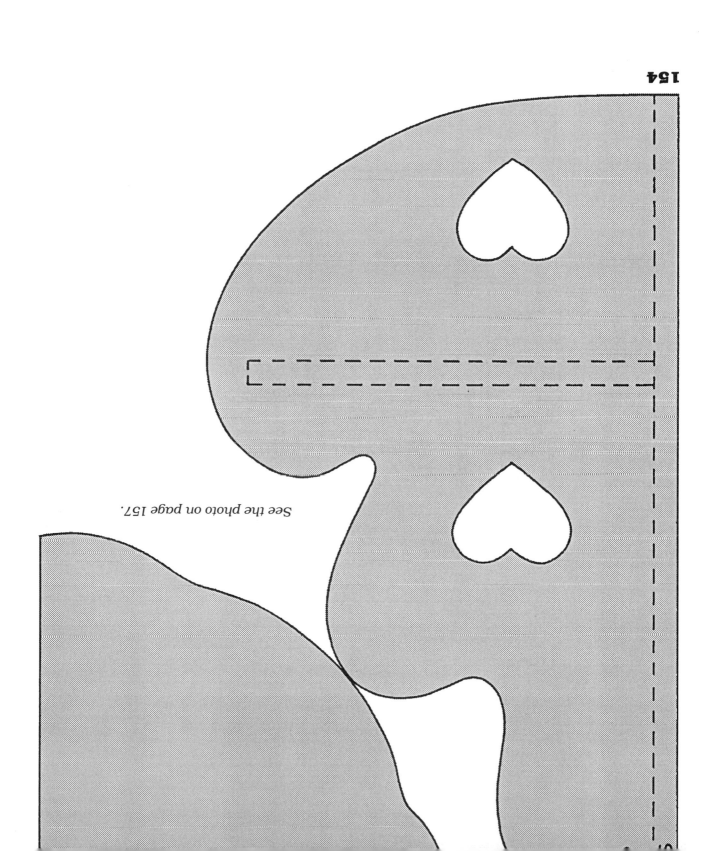

See the photo on page 157.

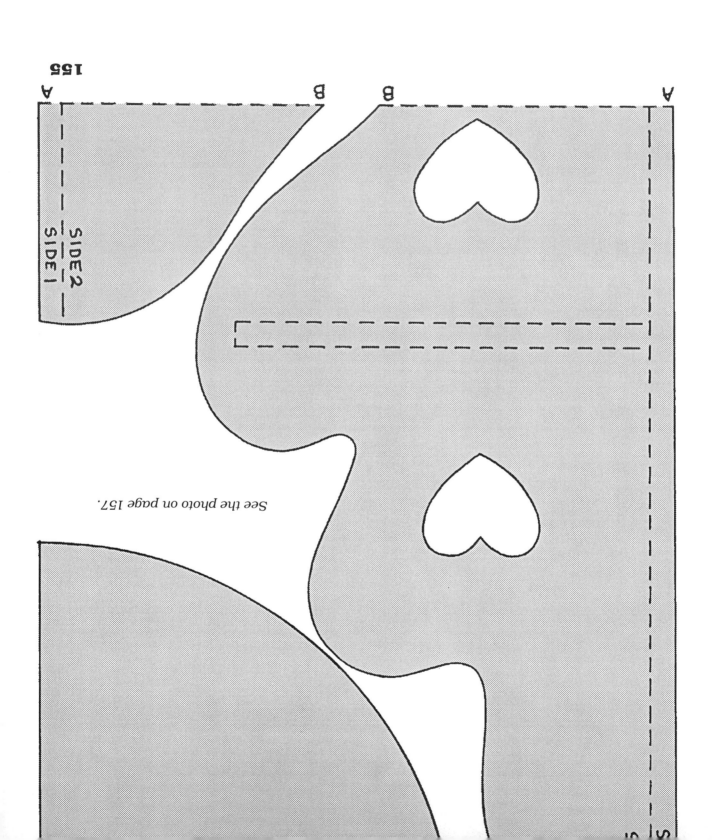

SIDE 2
SIDE 1

See the photo on page 157.

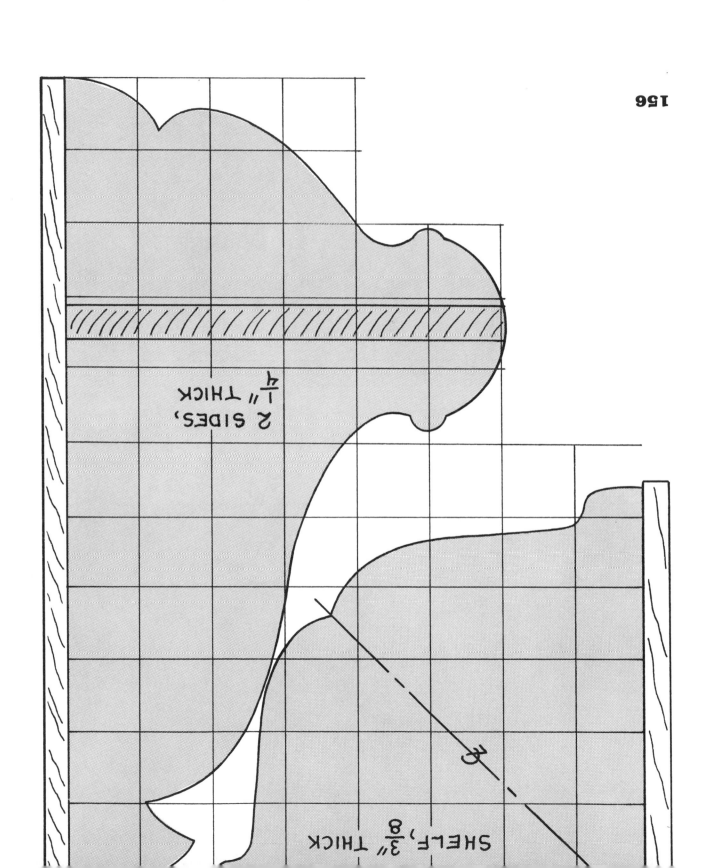

2 SIDES, $\frac{1}{4}"$ THICK

3

SHELF, $\frac{3}{8}"$ THICK

This small corner shelf would also look good in larger sizes.

Letter holder/key rack made from ¼" plywood.

A small corner shelf made of ¼" walnut

157

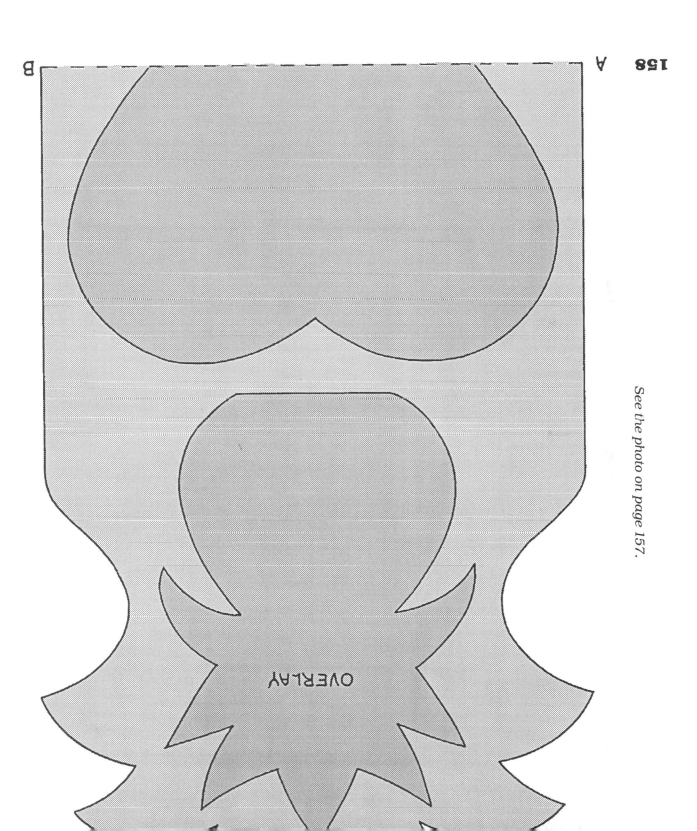

OVERLAY

See the photo on page 157.

See the photo on page 157.

TYPICAL
SIDE VIEW DETAIL

1/2"

20°

See page A of the color section.

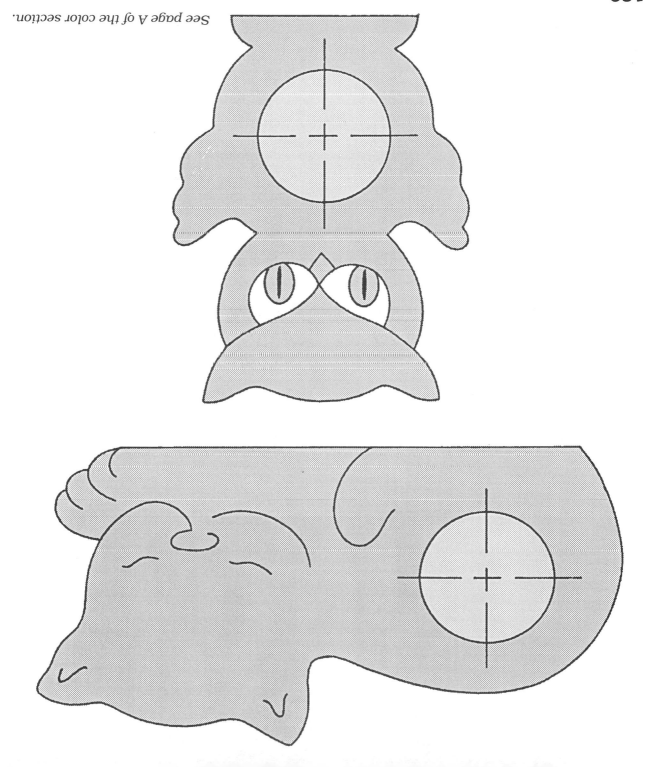

Quartz miniclocks in small solid-wood cutouts sawn from ¾"-thick stock. See page A of the color section.

A hen clock with a sponge-technique finish highlighted with individual dots, applied with the tip of a brush handle. See page H of the color section.

A hanging goose clock. See page H of the color section.

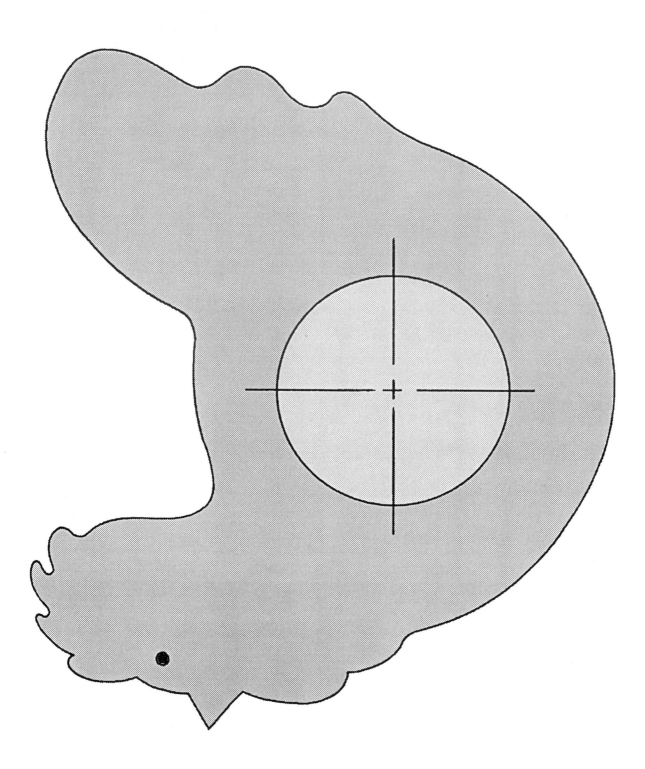

*This project needs a clock with a 2¹³⁄₁₆″ diameter face that fits into a 2³⁄₈″ diameter opening.
See the photos on page 161 and page H of the color section.*

162

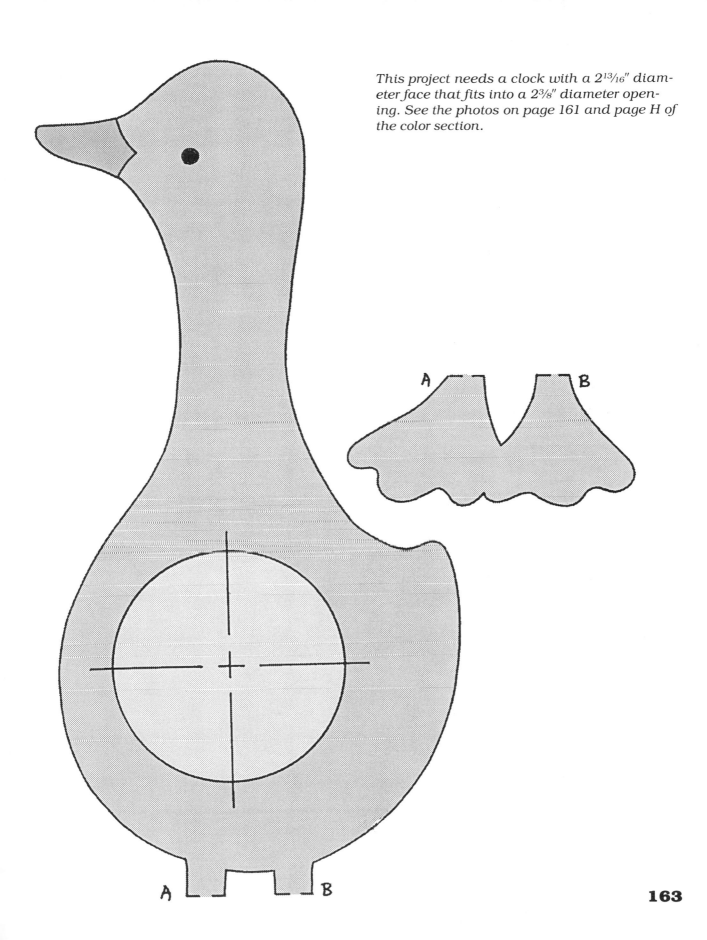

This project needs a clock with a 2¹³⁄₁₆″ diameter face that fits into a 2⅜″ diameter opening. See the photos on page 161 and page H of the color section.

A

B

A

B

A

B

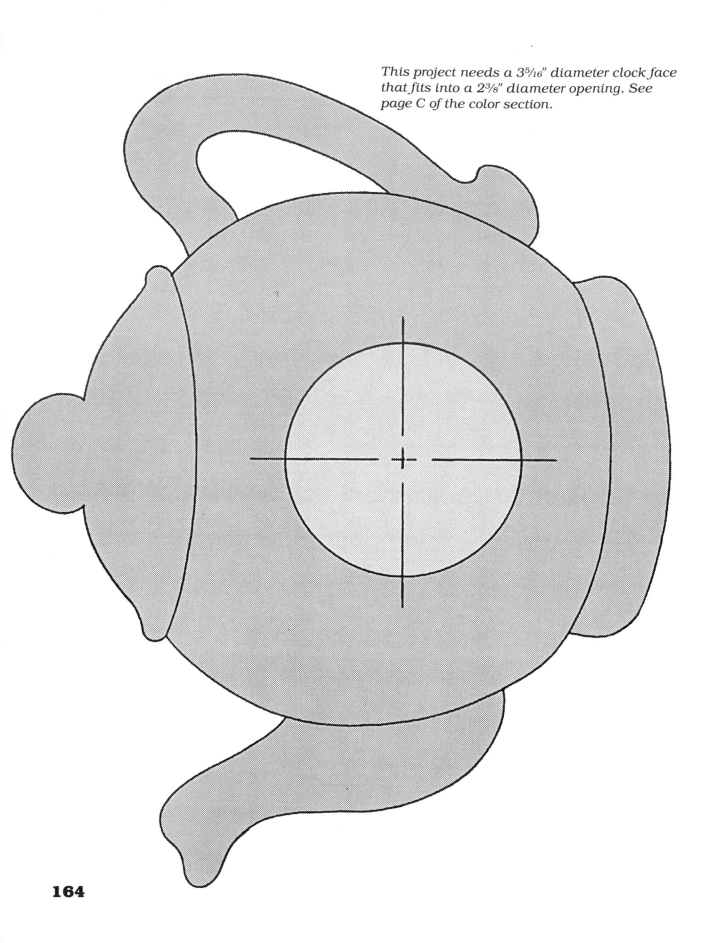

This project needs a 3⁵⁄₁₆″ diameter clock face that fits into a 2³⁄₈″ diameter opening. See page C of the color section.

164

A segmented teapot. See page C of the color section.

Goose thermometer. See page H of the color section.

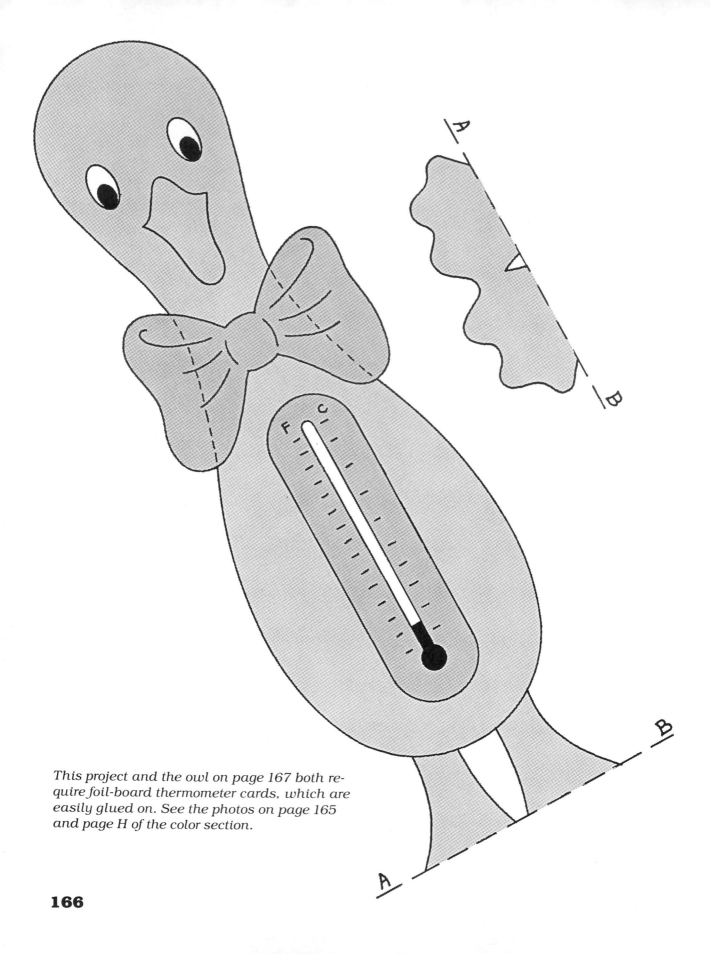

This project and the owl on page 167 both require foil-board thermometer cards, which are easily glued on. See the photos on page 165 and page H of the color section.

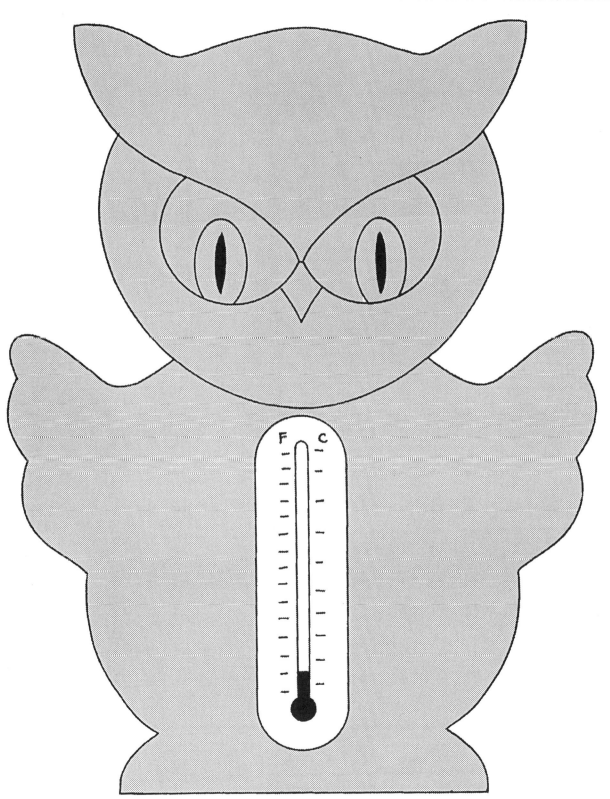

167

Picture Frames

$\frac{3}{8}'' \times \frac{3}{8}''$ REAR RABBET

Picture frames are cut from ¾″-thick stock and rabbeted with a router. See page E of the color section.

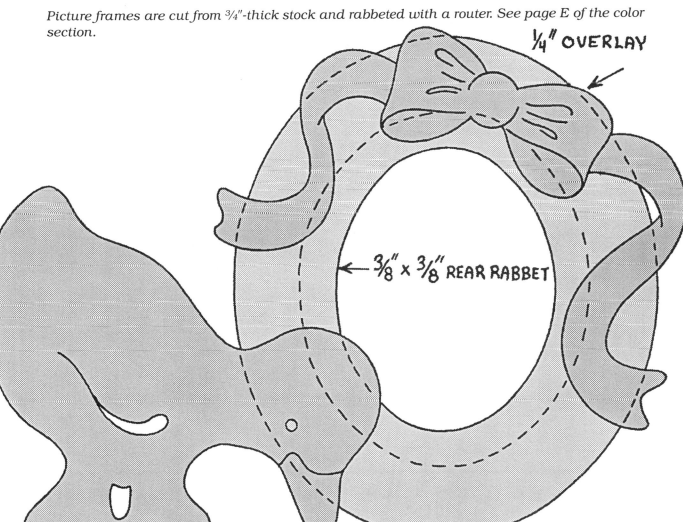

¼″ OVERLAY

⅜″ x ⅜″ REAR RABBET

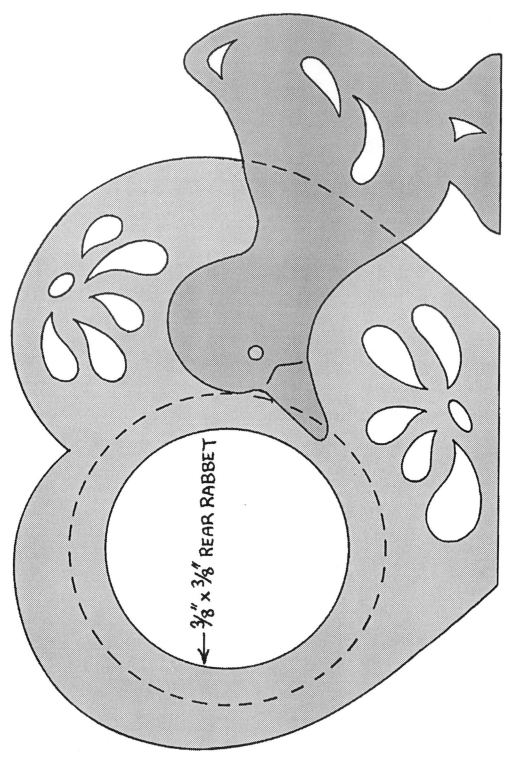

3/8" x 3/8" REAR RABBET

See the photos on page 169 and page E of the color section.

Fretted hen cutout made from ¾" thick material

This swan silhouette can be cut from any thickness material. See page E of the color section.

A corner window silhouette cut from thin plywood. See page E of the color section.

A goose window/wall hanging cut from plywood. See page E of the color section.

172

173

See the photos on page 172 and page E of the color section.

174

See the photos on page 172 and page E of the
color section.

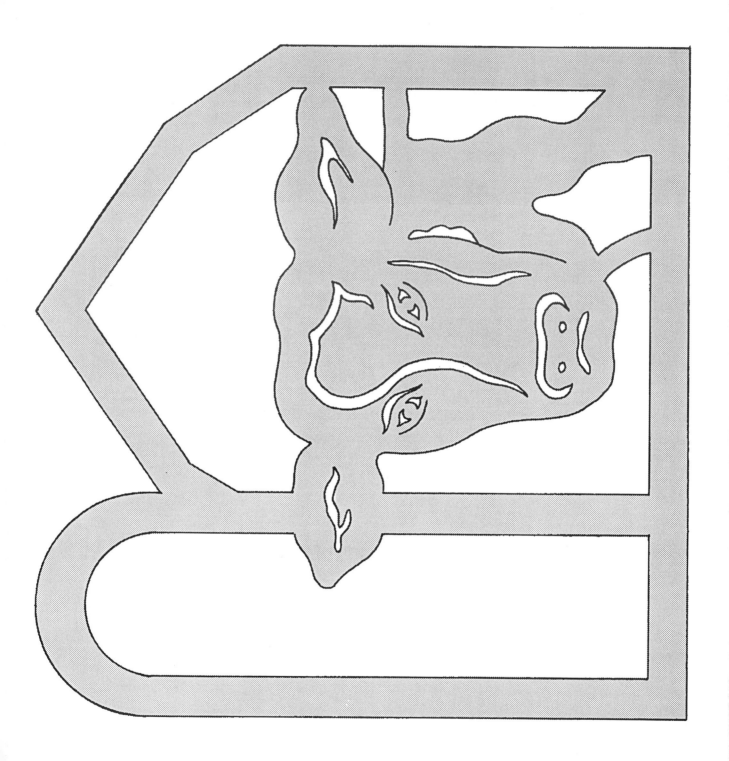

176

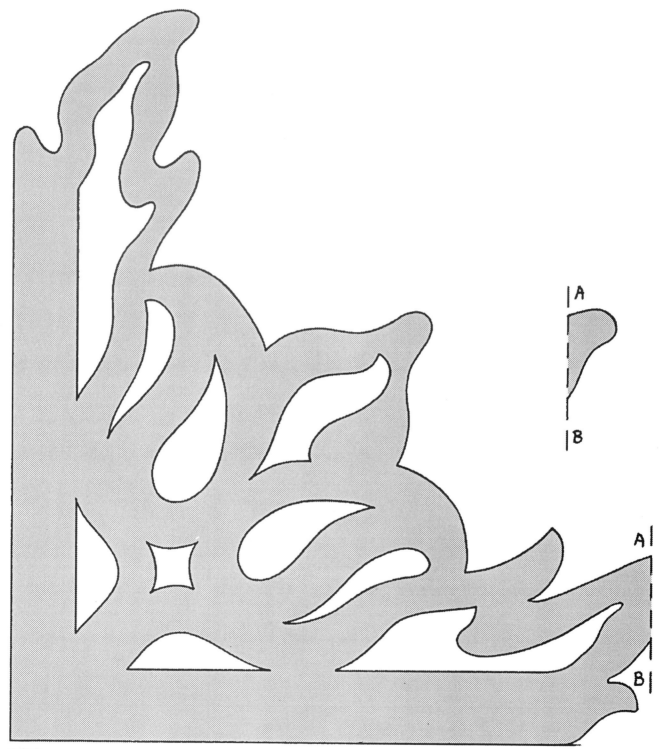

A

B

A

B

178

179

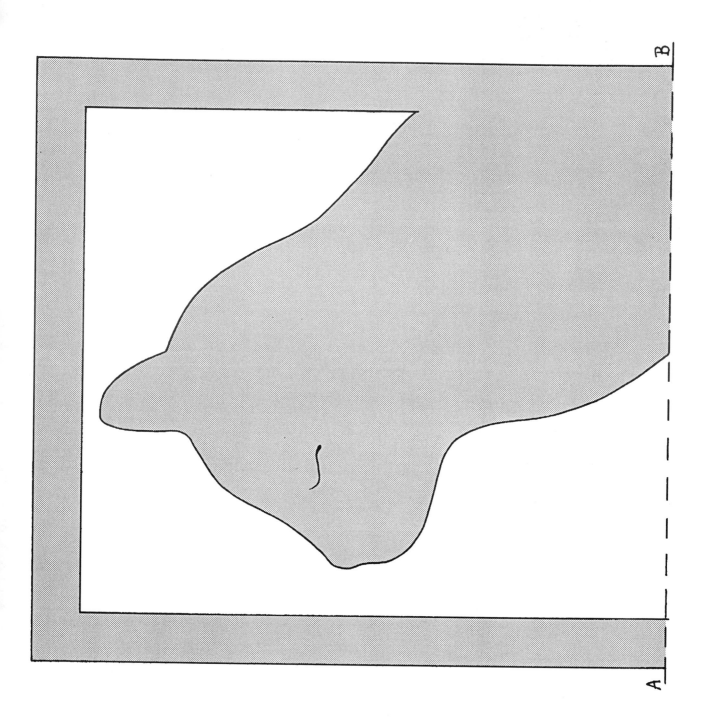

A

B

180

Numbers cut from ¾″-thick solid wood. See the pattern on page 184, and the photo on page H of the color section.

Sawn Pictures with Overlays

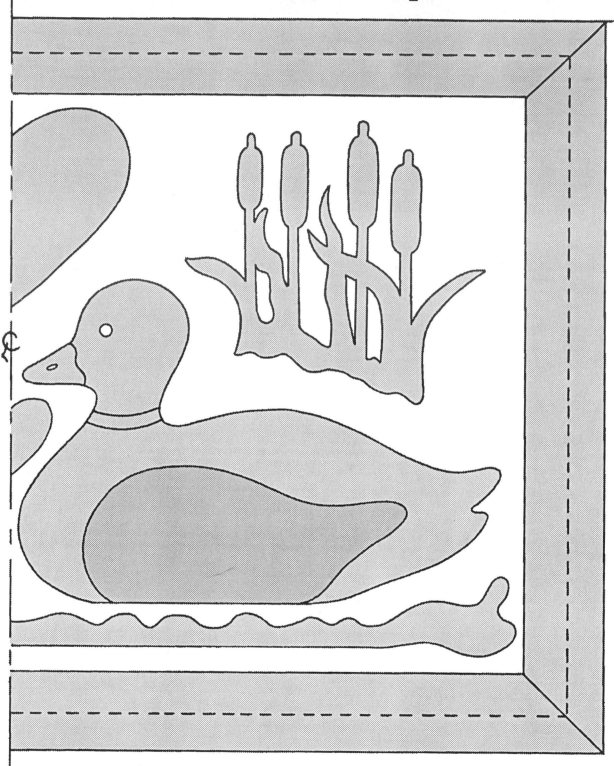

Half-pattern shown with an optional frame. See the photo on page 191.

Half-pattern shown with an optional frame.

Alphabet & Numbers

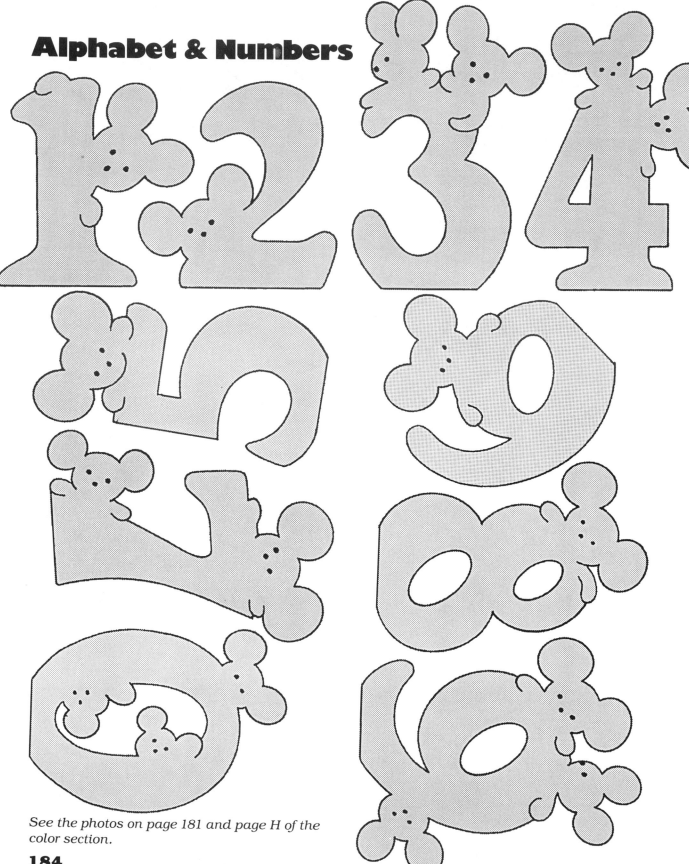

See the photos on page 181 and page H of the color section.

184

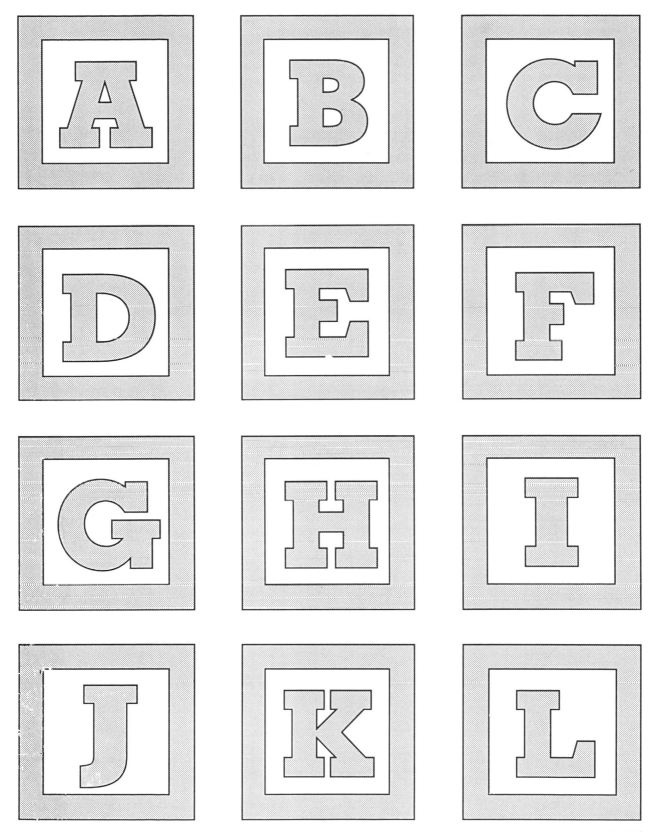

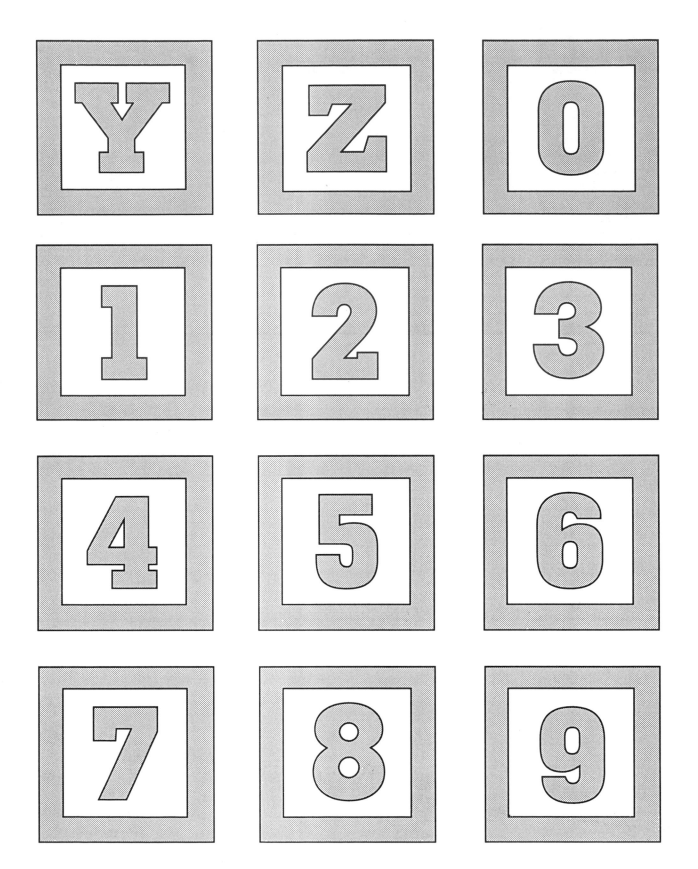

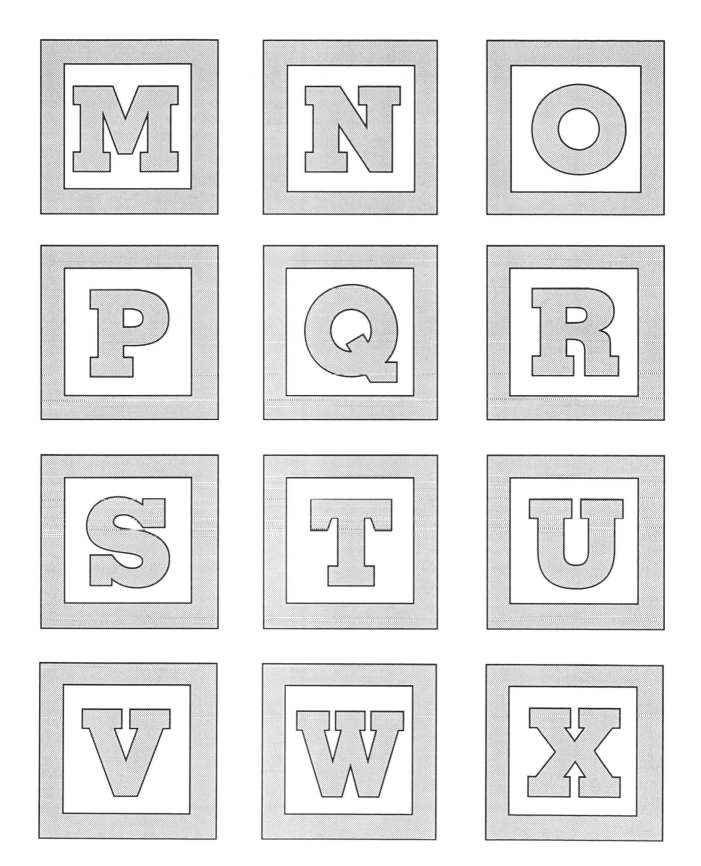

Current Books by Patrick Spielman

Carving Wild Animals: Life-Size Wood Figures. Spielman and renowned woodcarver Bill Dehos show how to carve more than 20 magnificent creatures of the North American wild. A cougar, black bear, prairie dog, squirrel, raccoon, and fox are some of the life-size animals included. Step-by-step, photo-filled instructions and multiple-view patterns, plus tips on the use of tools, wood selection, finishing, and polishing, help bring each animal to life. Oversized. Over 300 photos. 16 pages in full color. 240 pages.

Christmas Scroll Saw Patterns. Patrick and Patricia Spielman provide over 200 original, full-size scroll saw patterns with Christmas as the theme, including: toys, shelves, tree, window, and table decorations; segmented projects; and alphabets. A wide variety of Santas, trees, and holiday animals are included, as is a short, illustrated review of scroll saw techniques. 4 pages in color. 164 pages.

Classic Fretwork Scroll Saw Patterns. Spielman and coauthor James Reidle provide over 140 imaginative patterns inspired by and derived from mid- to late-19th-century scroll-saw masters. This book covers nearly 30 categories of patterns and includes a brief review of scroll-saw techniques and how to work with patterns. The patterns include ornamental numbers and letters, beautiful birds, signs, wall pockets, silhouettes, a sleigh, jewelry boxes, toy furniture, and more. 192 pages.

Country Mailboxes. Spielman and co-author Paul Meisel have come up with the 20 best country-style mailbox designs. They include an old pump fire wagon, a Western saddle, a Dalmatian, and even a boy fishing. Simple instructions cover cutting, painting, decorating, and installation. Over 200 illustrations. 4 pages in color. 164 pages.

Gluing & Clamping. A thorough, up-to-date examination of one of the most critical steps in woodworking. Spielman explores the features of every type of glue—from traditional animal-hide glues to the newest epoxies—the clamps and tools needed, the bonding properties of different wood species, safety tips, and all techniques from edge-to-edge and end-to-end gluing to applying plastic laminates. Also included is a glossary of terms. Over 500 illustrations. 256 pages.

Making Country-Rustic Wood Projects. Hundreds of photos, patterns, and detailed scaled drawings reveal construction methods, woodworking techniques, and Spielman's professional secrets for making indoor and outdoor furniture in the distinctly attractive Country-Rustic style. Covered are all aspects of furniture making from choosing the best wood for the job to texturing smooth boards. Among the dozens of projects are mailboxes, cabinets, shelves, coffee tables, weather vanes, doors, panelling, plant stands, and many other durable and economical pieces. 400 illustrations. 4 pages in color. 164 pages.

Making Wood Bowls with a Router & Scroll Saw. Using scroll-sawn rings, inlays, fretted edges, and much more, Spielman and master craftsman Carl Roehl have developed a completely new approach to creating decorative bowls. Over 200 illustrations. 8 pages in color. 168 pages.

Making Wood Decoys. This clear, step-by-step approach to the basics of decoy carving is abundantly illustrated with close-up photos for designing, selecting, and obtaining woods; tools; feather detailing; painting; and finishing of decorative and working decoys. Six different professional decoy artists are featured. Photo gallery (4 pages in full color) along with numerous detailed plans for various popular decoys. 164 pages.

Making Wood Signs. Designing, selecting woods and tools, and every process through finishing clearly covered. Instructions for hand- and power-carving, routing, and sandblasting techniques for small to huge signs. Foolproof guides for professional letters and ornaments. Hundreds of photos (4 pages in full color). Lists sources for supplies and special tooling. 148 pages.

New Router Handbook. This updated and expanded version of the definitive guide to routing continues to revolutionize router use. The text, with over 1,000 illustrations, covers familiar and new routers, bits, accessories, and tables available today; complete maintenance and safety techniques; a multitude of techniques for both hand-held and mounted routers; plus dozens of helpful shop-made fixtures and jigs. 384 pages.

Original Scroll Saw Shelf Patterns. Patrick Spielman and Loren Raty provide over 50 original, full-size patterns for wall shelves, which may be copied applied directly to wood. Photographs of finished shelves are included, as well as in formation on choosing woods, stack sawing, and finishing. 4 pages in color. 132 pages.

Realistic Decoys. Spielman and master carver Keith Bridenhagen reveal their successful techniques for carving, feather texturing, painting, and finishing wood decoys. Details you can't find elsewhere—anatomy, attitudes, markings, and the easy, step-by-step approach to perfect delicate procedures—make this book invaluable. Includes listings for contests, shows, and sources of tools and supplies. 274 close-up photos. 8 pages in color. 232 pages.

Router Basics. With over 200 close-up, step-by-step photos and drawings, this valuable starter handbook will guide the new owner, as well as provide a spark to owners for whom the router isn't the tool they turn to most often. Covers all the basic router styles, along with how-it-works descriptions of all its major features. Includes sections on bits and accesso-

ries, as well as square-cutting and trimming, case and furniture routing, cutting circles and arcs, template and freehand routing, and using the router with a router table. 128 pages.

Router Jigs & Techniques. A practical encyclopedia of information, covering the latest equipment to use with the router, it describes all the newest commercial routing machines, along with jigs, bits, and other aids and devices. The book not only provides invaluable tips on how to determine which router and bits to buy, it explains how to get the most out of the equipment once it is bought. Over 800 photos and illustrations. 384 pages.

Scroll Saw Basics. Features more than 275 illustrations covering basic techniques and accessories. Sections include types of saws, features, selection of blades, safety, and how to use patterns. Half a dozen patterns are included to help the scroll saw user get started. Basic cutting techniques are covered, including inside cuts, bevel cuts, stack-sawing, and others. 128 pages.

Scroll Saw Country Patterns. With 300 full-size patterns in 28 categories, this selection of projects covers an extraordinary range, with instructions every step of the way. Projects include farm animals, people, birds, and butterflies, plus letter and key holders, coasters, switch plates, country hearts, and more. Directions for piercing, drilling, sanding, and finishing, as well as tips on using special tools. 4 pages in color. 196 pages.

Scroll Saw Fretwork Patterns. This companion book to *Scroll Saw Fretwork Techniques & Projects* features over 200 fabulous, full-size fretwork patterns. These patterns include popular classic designs, plus an array of imaginative contemporary ones. Choose from a variety of numbers, signs, brackets, animals, miniatures, and silhouettes, and more. 256 pages.

Scroll Saw Fretwork Techniques & Projects. A study in the historical development of fretwork, as well as the tools, techniques, materials, and project styles that have evolved over the past 130 years. Every intricate

189

turn and cut is explained, with over 550 step-by-step photos and illustrations. 32 projects are shown in full color. The book also covers some modern scroll sawing machines as well as state-of-the-art fretwork and fine scroll-sawing techniques. 8 pages in color. 232 pages.

Scroll Saw Handbook. The workshop manual to this versatile tool includes the basics (how scroll saws work, blades to use, etc.) and the advantages and disadvantages of the general types and specific brand-name models on the market. All cutting techniques are detailed, including compound and bevel sawing, making inlays, reliefs, and recesses, cutting metals and other non-woods, and marquetry. There's even a section on transferring patterns to wood. Over 500 illustrations. 256 pages.

Scroll Saw Holiday Patterns. Patrick and Patricia Spielman provide over 100 full-size, shaded patterns for easy cutting, plus full-color photos of projects. Will serve all your holiday pleasures—all year long. Use these holiday patterns to create decorations, centerpieces, mailboxes, and diverse projects to keep or give as gifts. Standard holidays, as well as the four seasons, birthdays, and anniversaries, are represented. 8 pages of color. 168 pages.

Scroll Saw Pattern Book. The original classic pattern book—over 450 patterns for wall plaques, refrigerator magnets, candle holders, pegboards, jewelry, ornaments, shelves, brackets, picture frames, signboards, and many other projects. Beginning and experienced scroll saw users alike will find something to intrigue and challenge them. 256 pages.

Scroll Saw Puzzle Patterns. 80 full-size patterns for jigsaw puzzles, stand-up puzzles, and inlay puzzles. With meticulous attention to detail, Patrick and Patricia Spielman provide instructions and step-by-step photos, along with tips on tools and wood selection, for making dinosaurs, camels, hippopotami, alligators—even a family of elephants! Inlay puzzle patterns include basic shapes, numbers, an accurate piece-together map of the United States, and a host of other colorful edu-

cational and enjoyable games for children. 8 pages of color. 264 pages.

Scroll Saw Shelf Patterns. Spielman and Loren Raty offer full-size patterns for 44 different shelf styles. Designs include wall shelves, corner shelves, and multi-tiered shelves. The patterns work well with ¼-inch hardwood, plywood or any solid wood. Over 150 illustrations. 4 pages in color. 132 pages.

Scroll Saw Silhouette Patterns. With over 120 designs, Spielman and James Reidle provide an extremely diverse collection of intricate silhouette patterns, ranging from Victorian themes to sports to cowboys. They also include mammals, birds, country and nautical designs, as well as dragons, cars, and Christmas themes. Tips, hints, and advice are included along with detailed photos of finished works. 160 pages.

Sharpening Basics. The ultimate handbook that goes well beyond the "basics," to become the major up-to-date reference work features more than 300 detailed illustrations (mostly photos) explaining every facet of tool sharpening. Sections include bench-sharpening tools, sharpening machines, and safety. Chapters cover cleaning tools, and sharpening all sorts of tools, including chisels, plane blades (irons), hand knives, carving tools, turning tools, drill and boring tools, router and shaper tools, jointer and planer knives, screwdrivers and scrapers, and, of course, saws. 128 pages.

Spielman's Original Scroll Saw Patterns. 262 full-size patterns that don't appear elsewhere feature teddy bears, dinosaurs, sports figures, dancers, cowboy cutouts, Christmas ornaments, and dozens more. Fretwork patterns are included for a Viking ship, framed cutouts, wall-hangers, key-chain miniatures, jewelry, and much more. Hundreds of step-by-step photos and drawings show how to turn, repeat, and crop each design for thousands of variations. 4 pages of color. 228 pages.

Victorian Gingerbread: Patterns & Techniques. Authentic pattern designs (many full-size) cover the full range of indoor and outdoor detailing: brackets, corbels, shelves, grilles, spandrels, balusters, running trim, headers, valances, gable ornaments, screen doors, pickets, trellises, and much more. Also included are complete plans for Victorian mailboxes, house numbers, signs, and more. With clear instructions and helpful drawings, the book also provides tips for making gingerbread trim. 8 pages in color. 200 pages.

Victorian Scroll Saw Patterns. Intricate original designs plus classics from the 19th century are presented in full-size, shaded patterns. Instructions are provided with drawings and photos. Projects include alphabets and numbers, silhouettes and designs for shelves, frames, filigree baskets, plant holders, decorative boxes, picture frames, welcome signs, architectural ornaments, and much more. 160 pages.

Working Green Wood with PEG. Covers every process for making beautiful, inexpensive projects from green wood without cracking, splitting, or warping it. Hundreds of clear photos and drawings show every step from obtaining the raw wood through shaping, treating, and finishing PEG-treated projects. 175 unusual project ideas. Lists supply sources. 120 pages.

Plaque components are sawn from ⅛"-thick solid stock or plywoods, stack-sawn to simplify duplication. See page E of the color section, and the pattern on page 182.

Index